Twayne's United States Authors Series

Sylvia E. Bowman, *Editor*

INDIANA UNIVERSITY

Joseph Kirkland

JOSEPH KIRKLAND

by CLYDE E. HENSON

Twayne Publishers, Inc.   ::   New York

MANUFACTURED IN THE UNITED STATES OF AMERICA BY
UNITED PRINTING SERVICES, INC.
NEW HAVEN, CONN.

FOR MARY

Preface

JOSEPH KIRKLAND'S place in the literary history of the United States has been assured by the historians of the past. His reputation rests principally on his novel of Western life, *Zury: The Meanest Man in Spring County*, in which, as William Dean Howells pointed out, Kirkland created a new type of character: the money-grabbing, land-grabbing, mortgage-holding farmer who devotes all his energies to the acquisition of wealth. Kirkland also experimented with the frank treatment of sex in a period when literary convention dared go no further than the kiss or the embrace. He was a realist who intended to portray life as he saw it.

In this work I have been concerned with the aspects of Kirkland's life which influenced his writing; I have, therefore, organized the material on a chronological basis. I have not tried to write a definitive biography, but I have used biography to approach Kirkland's work and its meaning. I have not been concerned with sociological criticism, and I have not rejected historical scholarship in my attempt to look honestly at Kirkland's novels.

In the chapters about the novels, I have treated them in the order in which they were written, which is also the order of their importance. Kirkland's second novel, *The McVeys* has much less to say than *Zury; The Captain of Company K* has much less to say than *The McVeys*. *Zury*, therefore, is accorded more space in my treatment; but I have necessarily repeated some of the material about style, plot, character, methods, and meanings, for each novel is considered separately. The histories are principally period pieces; they are of interest to someone who is interested in Kirkland. I have treated them accordingly; they are not great histories any more than Kirkland's novels are great novels.

Kirkland is not a great literary figure: his powers were too limited, and he himself knew it. He started too late, but he contributed to the larger pattern of realism as a literary theory and practice. His true significance is that he was a pioneer realist in Chicago at a time when that city was becoming a center of literary activity; and, to the younger writers, he was the first professional man of letters in the city. His apparent success encouraged them to continue their efforts to write fiction of the highest order.

My first study of Kirkland was completed under the guidance of Professor Lyon N. Richardson, Western Reserve University; it is a pleasure to record my appreciation to him and to the Committee on American Culture.

I am indebted to Western Reserve University, Michigan State University, and the Rockefeller Foundation Mid-western Studies Fund for financial aid during the original study. I am grateful to Michigan State University for a grant for the preparation of the manuscript of this work.

I must thank Dr. Stanley Pargellis, Director, the Newberry Library, Chicago, Illinois, for permission to use the materials in the Kirkland Papers; Professor Eldon C. Hill for copies of the Kirkland–Garland correspondence which he made with Garland's permission when the letters were in his possession sometime before Garland's death; Miss Winifred Wilson, Evanston, Illinois, for permission to use the numerous items in her possession, especially the records of conversations which she had with Kirkland's daughter Louise; the Macmillan Company for permission to quote from Hamlin Garland's *Roadside Meetings* and *A Son of the Middle Border;* Miss Margaret Flint, Illinois State Historical Society Library, Springfield, Illinois; the librarians at Western Reserve University, the University of Chicago, and Michigan State University; and my colleagues in the Department of English, Michigan State University.

CLYDE E. HENSON

East Lansing
April 15, 1961

Contents

Chronology

1830   Joseph Kirkland born on January 7; the son of William and Caroline Kirkland.

1835-
1843   Moved with parents to Detroit, Michigan, and in 1837, to Pinckney, Michigan, where his mother began to write sketches of frontier life.

1843   Returned to New York with family.

1846   Accidental death of father on October 18.

1847   July 1, Kirkland a sailor on packet between United States and England; visited his uncle Joseph Stansbury in England.

1852   Clerk and reader in offices of *Putnam's Monthly Magazine.*

1855-
1858   Moved to Chicago; traveled as an auditor for Illinois Central Railroad.

1858   Settled at Tilton, Illinois; supervisor with Carbon Coal Company.

1860   Member of committee to inform Lincoln of his nomination for the presidency.

1861   On April 25, enlisted in Company C, Illinois Twelfth Regiment; elected lieutenant; promoted to captain, August 26. Made aide-de-camp to General McClellan. Aide-de-camp in Adjutant General's Department, Washington, D. C., November 1; became acquainted with John Hay and John Nicolay and renewed acquaintance with President Lincoln.

1862-
1863   Staff of Fitz-John Porter. Breveted major. General Burnside's staff.

1863   Resigned from Army on February 22, effective January 7; returned to Tilton. Married Theodosia Burr Wilkinson, daughter of John Wilkinson, of Syracuse, New York; established coal mining operations at Tilton.

1864   Death of his mother, Caroline Kirkland; first issue of *The Prairie Chicken.*

1867   Trip to Europe with family.

1868   Moved to Huron Street, Chicago; established retail coal business.

1871   Coal business destroyed by fire; built new house on corner of Rush and Superior streets.

1873   Entered Internal Revenue Department; studied law with Judge Mark Bangs.

1877   Filed bankruptcy, February 7; continued study of law.

1880   First in his class in bar examination; made partner in firm of Judge Mark Bangs. Wrote play, *The Married Flirt,* which failed.

1886   Reviewed Tolstoi's *War and Peace;* miscellaneous writings; work on first novel.

1887   Publication of *Zury: The Meanest Man in Spring County.*

1888   Publication of *The McVeys: An Episode.*

1889   Literary editor of Chicago *Tribune.*

1890-
1891   *The Captain of Company K* published serially in Detroit *Free Press* and in book form.

1891   Trip to Nicaragua; publication of *The Story of Chicago.*

1893   Member of the Committee on the World Exposition, Chicago.

1893   Publication of *The Chicago Massacre of 1812.*

1893   With John Moses, editor of *History of Chicago;* died from heart attack April 28, before work as editor completed; work finished by daughter Caroline.

1895   Publication of the two-volume *History of Chicago.*

Joseph Kirkland

CHAPTER 1

The Beginnings of Rustic Knowledge

AT SIXTY-FOUR, Joseph Kirkland had his career cut short by a fatal heart attack. He had filled the last years of his life with much literary activity; and, although his final work was the writing of history, he followed his desire to report life in fiction as realistically as he could. Lamenting that he had not been able to devote more years to writing fiction, he remarked to Hamlin Garland: "I started too late and lost the ability to emotionalize what I remembered."[1] Although he spent less than ten years producing fiction, Kirkland established himself as a novelist of considerable historical importance, becoming, as Hobart Chatfield-Taylor later wrote to Winifred Wilson, the "first professional literary man in Chicago."[2] More important, he led the way for Hamlin Garland, whose early work in fiction and poetry he criticized and revised before its publication; and Kirkland not only produced in his own work, as Garland asserted, the "truest fiction of the mid-West"[3] but also encouraged other authors to write realistically.

Historically, as a pioneer realist of the Middle Border, Joseph Kirkland continued the work which his mother had started with her sketches of frontier life in Michigan. His claim to remembrance is as a realist; for, his life nearly spent before he could fulfill an aim which he had had from childhood, Joseph Kirkland knew that the physical environments of his life gave impetus to his urge to write and that they supplied him with the material from which he would create his novels.

The external events of a man's life may not always be so significant as the history of his inner spirit; but the public events of Kirkland's life cannot be dismissed as entirely irrelevant to his work, for he wrote as a realist primarily from direct observation and memory. Joseph Kirkland—as well as his mother, Caroline Matilda Kirkland—wrote in opposition to the romanticism of an earlier age; he followed Hippolyte Taine's dictum to write about what he found in his own surroundings. And by the use of that environment, Kirkland helped create a sense of belonging to his own times and to a native way of life which formed the very heart of a mature, healthy literature in the United States. Because the events of his life form the basis of Kirkland's work, they must be set forth in some detail if his fiction is to be examined clearly.

Joseph Kirkland was born January 7, 1830, in Geneva, New York, where his parents, Caroline Stansbury and William Kirkland had recently established a school for girls. Both parents were members of families which had been active in the Revolutionary War; the Stansburys were Philadelphia loyalists and Anglican in religion; the Kirklands, New England patriots and Congregationalists.

William Kirkland attended Hamilton College, which had been founded by his uncle, Samuel; and then to prepare for the chair of languages, he had gone to Göttingen to the University.[4] When he returned, he and Caroline married and settled at Hamilton College until an accident impaired William's hearing. They then established a school at Geneva, New York; but, when it earned little money, the Kirklands looked elsewhere for means to increase their earnings. When, therefore, they were offered an opportunity to go to Detroit, Michigan, to take charge of a school, they accepted it. They intended, however, to support themselves by teaching only until they could find a place to begin a venture in land in the territory. Accordingly, in the summer of 1835, the Kirkland family left New York for Michigan and became a part of the land rush to the peninsula which reached its greatest proportions between 1830 and 1840, a decade in which the population increased from 31,000 to 212,000. The move provided Caroline Matilda Kirkland with the material for her realistic sketches of frontier life, and it brought to Joseph Kirkland an opportunity to observe and to participate in the life of a frontier community and to begin his awareness of dialect and of customs in a frontier farming community. The move, an experience common to the westward movement, was recorded by Caroline in her sketches of western life.

I Frontier Michigan

The optimism of the people of the Atlantic Seaboard which arose after the War of 1812 reached its height about the middle of the nineteenth century; and though the westward movement had long been a reality, the increasing current of migration carried thousands of settlers into the Old Northwest to settle in western Ohio, Indiana, Illinois, Wisconsin, and Michigan. National attention had been focused on Michigan in 1812 when Detroit was forced to surrender to the British; but then a combination of factors blocked the settlement of the territory until after Ohio, Indiana, and Illinois had been settled.

Natural barriers—the Great Lakes, swamps, and forests—prevented a landward approach to the peninsular region; and western New York, the natural source of supplies for settlers, was a wilderness. The result was that bounty lands to soldiers, as Kirkland noted in his first novel, were located in Indiana or Illinois. Michigan, therefore, remained unsettled until transportation difficulties were solved. The opening of the Erie Canal in 1825 and the development of the steamboats (the *Walk-in-the-Water* made its first voyage on Lake Erie in 1818) made available an all-water route to Michigan. In 1838 John T. Blois reported in his *Gazetteer of Michigan* that 200,000 settlers in search of land had passed through the port of Detroit.

The Kirklands traveled by water route from New York to Detroit, and along the lane of travel they saw colorful posters displayed in the taverns and heard talk of new cities being planned in the wilderness. Caroline recorded her impressions of how traffic in land was conducted by the "land sharks":

> When lots were to be sold, the whole fair dream was splendidly emblazoned on a sheet of super-royal size; things which only floated before the mind's eye of the most sanguine, were portrayed with bewitching minuteness for the delectation of

the ordinary observer. Majestic steamers plied their paddles to and fro upon the river; ladies crowding their decks and streamers floating upon the wind. Sloops dotted the harbors, while noble ships were seen in the offing. Mills, factories, and lighthouses—canals, railroads and bridges, all took their appropriate positions. Then came the advertisements, choicely worded, and carefully vague, never setting forth anything which might not come true at some time or other, yet leaving the buyer without excuse if he chose to be taken in.[5]

The lure of cheap land and the dream of paradise caught and held the settlers—even as it captured the Kirklands until the realities of life brought hardship and disillusionment.

Detroit, the destination of the Kirkland family, was not only the center of all the speculation activity in western lands in Michigan but also the gateway to El Dorado beyond. The narrow streets of the old village, deep in mud at most seasons of the year and impassable to everything except high two-wheeled French carts, were crowded beyond capacity. Taverns were filled; sleeping places sold at fabulously high prices. Food was poor and expensive. But the land fever took hold of everyone: "The tradesman forsook his shop; the farmer his plow; the merchant his counter; the lawyer his office; the minister his desk, to join the general chase."[6]

William Kirkland caught the land fever. When the family was settled in the brick building which was to house the school he had come to manage, he looked around for an opportunity to acquire acreage. He made several trips into the interior and, after a time, settled on an area in Livingstone County, where he began to buy land in January, 1836. By September, 1836, he, or relatives whom he had persuaded to join him in the venture, had acquired nearly 1,500 acres. He made plans to build a mill, to lay out a village, to become a rich and powerful country squire who would be at the top of the social structure.

The Kirkland land lay sixty miles from Detroit just south of the new Grand River Road and just eleven miles from the present city of Howell, Michigan. The rolling countryside was covered with oak trees and dotted with small reed-fringed lakes in the valleys. William decided to build his village on Portage Creek, two miles from Portage Lake, where he found a promising site for a mill. He laid out the village which was called Pinckney after his older brother, Charles Pinckney Kirkland, a lawyer in New York City; and he and the Kirkland family spent the fall and winter making preparations to go to the village. In the spring of 1837, with their possessions piled high in a wagon, the Kirklands—William and Caroline and three children, Elizabeth, Joseph, and Cordelia—left Detroit for their new home in the Michigan forests. Their last months in Detroit had not been happy ones: on March 8, Sara Kirkland, one of their children had fallen out of a window and had been killed on the pavement below; and on May 24, Elizabeth Stansbury, Caroline's mother, who had come to visit them, had died.

At the time the Kirklands left Detroit for their new home in the West, the Michigan territory was rapidly filling with settlers; and the interior of the territory could be reached by five principal roads. These had been laid out by the federal government as possible military routes and were marked by a blazed "H" on tree trunks. Most of them were little better than Indian trails which had been widened enough to permit wagon travel. The Chicago road passed within twelve miles of the Kirkland holdings in Livingstone County, and the Kirklands had used it in their earlier trips to the site of their proposed settlement. But a new road, the Grand River Road, led to Howell by way of the settlements of Redford, Farmington, and Kensington; and the Kirklands decided to use it. Caroline wrote in *A New Home—Who'll Follow?*: "We had taken a newly opened and somewhat lonely route this time, in deference to the opinion of those who ought to have known better, that this road from having been less traveled would not be quite so deep as the other . . ."[7] She then described the difficulties which they encountered because of the depth of the ruts in the road. Heavily loaded wagons, carrying all the possessions essential to the settler's lowly state, had cut ever-deepening ruts in the soft forest floor; and the ground, shaded for centuries, stored water which seeped into the ruts to form great pools of water and mud. Marshes and swamps were bridged by rolling, slippery logs forming what is commonly called a "corduroy road."

After the Kirklands left the Grand River trail, they had

to make their way across unmarked land; and they lost their way in a swamp. One of the horses mired in a marsh; cut loose, it got out of the mud and ran away. William rode to find a farmer who might have oxen that could pull the wagon through the swamp, and Caroline and the children stayed in the wagon. The sun was hot, the air was humid, the children were restless and thirsty. The surrounding grass, growing out of the water, would not support their weight; but they got water by creeping down the wagon tongue to a clear stream. The children made a game of getting water until one of them became incautious and fell into the swamp. But they got out of the swamp and moved on toward their new home, the site of the village of Pinckney.

They took temporary refuge in a cabin which had been built by a farmer some years before. At one end of the single room were two beds, curtained with cotton sheets pinned to the rafters. A chest was placed between the beds, and the Sunday wardrobe hung over the chest. The other end of the room had a great open hearth, flanked on one side by a cupboard and on the other by a stick ladder leading to the loft where there were home-made bedsteads with the bark still on the split logs from which they were made. Partitions, made from sheets gave some privacy, and the Kirklands covered the open window with quilts. The log walls, plastered with mud, were covered with broadsides, circus posters, and newspapers. The Kirklands lived in this cabin until they could build their own, a slightly larger one, which they finished and moved into in the late summer—just before William, the youngest son, was born. Joseph remembered this home well enough to describe it in *Zury* as that of the Prouders.

The Kirklands faced all the problems encountered in the building of a town. They found it difficult to get carpenters to work because frontiersmen worked only when they chose. They became involved in lawsuits over the rights to build a mill. They tried unsuccessfully to speed the transportation of brick from Detroit. They found that all things moved more slowly than they had anticipated. But finally, the plat of the village was recorded on August 9, 1837. The little town was the natural business center of two or three hundred families; and the flour mill, which soon started operation, brought all types of settlers into the village where they were observed by the alert Joseph. Joseph never forgot the experiences, and he drew upon them to portray the little town of Wayback in *Zury*.

The settlers in the deep forest were very active with building and clearing the land. The great trees were felled or girdled and left to die; and some were burned over, including the trees in the public square of the village, which, though Caroline tried to save them, were cut down leaving ugly stumps to rot in the heat of the summer's sun—and similar stumps rotted in the town of Wayback in Joseph's first novel. But with all their work, the earlier settlers were often short of supplies; they borrowed from anyone, simply because one person might have plenty while his neighbors had nothing. They quickly assumed that they were all equal, and they practiced the equality of social and economic status which the frontier forced upon all.

The fact was that the thousands who came to Michigan in the first fever of the land rush, with its speculation in advancing land prices, paid little attention to food. A long, hard process of clearing was necessary before the forest was ready for crops; roads leading from Detroit were frequently impassable; and Detroit itself was icebound for much of the year. As a result, during 1835 and 1836 food was scarce, expensive, and poor in quality. Milk, eggs, vegetables were almost unknown, but hard salt ham was available. It became the pioneer staple, as Joseph Kirkland was to note in his novels, for it remained edible in all weather and was full of nourishment. Sweets, except for maple sugar, were not easily found, and maple sugar was not much esteemed because of its color. Game was plentiful: deer, turkeys, ducks, pheasants, and grouse abounded. Rivers and lakes were full of fish; sturgeon weighing over a hundred pounds were caught in the Michigan rivers. And Indians brought in some food to swap, so that fresh berries and venison could be obtained from them.

The village prospered, however, and when the spring came in 1836, Caroline sent for her piano—and overwhelmed the villagers with the awe of unheard-of luxury, a reaction Joseph recorded in his novels. Moreover, the Kirklands, always deep-

ly interested in education, caused a crude schoolhouse to
be built of green, unplaned oak boards which quickly
warped, and through the large cracks the winter wind blew
the snow onto the floor. The school had a regular school-
master who boarded around in winter, but in summer the
school was kept by local girls, "school-ma'ams," with little
training.

The Kirklands sent Joseph to the local school; but they sent
Elizabeth, the eldest daughter, back to Utica, New York, to
get her schooling under the direction of Caroline's aunt,
Lydia Mott. But, in addition to his work at the local school,
Joseph learned Latin and other subjects at home; later he felt
that he had gained most of his education through "contact
with his brilliant mother."[9] As life became routine, the
Kirklands felt that at last they had found security; but just
as the village seemed on the way toward the fulfillment of
their expectations, the prosperous years ended.

As early as 1836 the country was entering a depression
caused by unregulated currency and overexpansion of credit.
To combat the inflation, President Jackson issued an order
directing all public officers to receive and to pay out only
coin, thus forcing the withdrawal of government funds from
depositories and making scarce the amount of specie available for circulation. Tight credit brought business in the
East to a standstill, but the full force of the depression was
not at once felt in Michigan where the settlers had ready
cash that they had brought with them. But such money was
rapidly used up, and the banks could no longer make specie
payments. When the banks of New York City refused to re-
deem their notes on May 10, 1837, the Detroit banks followed
their example; and land, so desirable a short time before, lost
its value. The ruin was made greater in 1839 by the collapse of the wildcat banks of Michigan. These banks had
operated under the General Banking Law of 1837; but, when
that law was declared unconstitutional in 1839, stockholders
and bankers were released from all liability incurred during
the period of time the law was in operation. The result was
chaos.

In Michigan the settlers were reduced to hunger and want
by the collapse of the banks. Famine, never far from the

cabins in the forest, came uncomfortably close. Seed corn and potatoes, the basis for the next year's crop, were consumed; fish speared from the rivers were cooked and eaten without salt or fat; distress and suffering were widespread; and poverty and hardship, which had been bravely endured as long as there was hope for the future, were bitterly resented by the settlers.

These hard times made a lasting impression upon eight-year-old Joseph Kirkland. He watched, remembered, and used his memories as examples in his novels and as illustrations in his histories. His father tried to borrow money, but he could find none available to him. And Caroline, in the hope of ameliorating the financial strain, decided to try to earn money with her pen. Drawing directly from her experiences on the frontier, she published her first work on western life, *A New Home—Who'll Follow?*, in 1839. Because she did not wish to be known to her neighbors, she published her work under the pen name of Mary Clavers.

Caroline Kirkland had a keen eye for her fellow man, and her pictures of frontier life and people were built from her own observations. In the preface she wrote that she wished to make her work a "veritable history; an unimpeachable transcript of reality; a rough picture, in detached parts, but pentagraphed from life; a sort of 'Emigrants' Guide.'"[10] She chose the "charming sketches of village life" of Mary Russell Mitford's *Our Village* (5 vols., 1824-1832), as her model; and she hoped that a series of informal, rambling essays and stories would allow her to comment about any subject which might suggest itself. Caroline meant to write of the life of Pinckney, Michigan, as she saw it; and she must have clarified her sight by reading and discussing her writing with her family.

In following her aim to make a "transcript of reality," she became a pioneer realist—and she impressed her son Joseph with the sense of art which took the low and commonplace as its subject and turned it by careful treatment into literature. The desire to try his own hand at writing was created by his mother's work, and he intended to follow her example of depicting what he saw.

Caroline's work was praised by critics; furthermore, it sold well. But in her devotion to the record of life in Pinckney she had drawn her characters so well that many of the towns-people recognized themselves, and they did not like the pictures she had presented. The temper of the community rose against her; and, though she published *Forest Life* in 1842 and claimed that all the characters in it were imagined, she found that her imaginary characters took on "angry reality": the enraged people of the community reached the point of threatening the Kirkland family. The unhappiness which the Kirkland family had found in Michigan not only increased under the pressure of the community but became unbearable.

Caroline's work had established her as a successful writer; she made more and more frequent trips to Detroit to attend to the business of publication and to undergo treatment for milk-leg. Little by little, she began to feel that she would like to return to New York City where she would not have to leave her family for long trips. Furthermore, New York was becoming the publishing center of the United States; and, living there, she could employ more gainfully her ability to write.

During the journeys to Detroit, she left the children at home. Joseph, now twelve (1842), was big enough to do useful tasks about the village; and he got a job delivering mail to and from the post office in Dexter, Michigan, some fifteen miles away. The ride gave him a chance to see the country and to observe the settlers in another village, and the work gave him a sense of responsibility which he was never to forget. Already he had learned that "business is business," and he trained himself in careful business habits. He worked at his lessons also, for his father and mother made sure that he learned his Latin, and he practiced the art of letter writing as well. He wrote to his sister Elizabeth in Utica, trying to give her a sense of the dialect of the local people. "My dear Lizzie," he wrote, in November, 1842,

> How glad I should be to see you home again, and I think it very probable that, although you have very pleasant times in Utica, you would "kinder like" to see home yourself. At least I judge so from your letter; which we received on Friday last. The new wagon arrived about an hour ago, and a very nice wagon it is, the box is green with large black figures on it. The wheels and under part are red. . . . Our school

began today. It is taught by Mr. Wilson who is going to move into the house Mr. Cook lived in, and Mr. C. is going into the house Mr. Stephens lived in. . . .

In February, 1843, he wrote again to Elizabeth:

We are all well at present except Mamma's leg which I believe is better than it use to be. I believe the country all around is uncommonly healthy as I hope it is around Utica. Hay is getting so scarce around here with the long winter that there is much danger of many cattle starving if spring does not come on soon, indeed Mr. Fasquelle says that many have almost starved *up north.* Meat and flour are still extremely cheap and are likely to be so, Papa says. Mrs. Wilson had a present of a barrel of flour, since Mr. W. went to Detroit, from Mr. John Porter.

Papa *got up* a wood-bee for Mrs. W. and got thereby seven loads of wood; which William [Joseph's brother] and I are trying how long it will take us to cut it up. I am going after I have learnt my Latin lesson, for Papa always makes me learn my lesson first and I have two lessons to learn in the day, so I make them into one long one; and what with bringing in the wood making fires eating my meals and many other things I do not generally get off till half after two o'clock and then I "put in" till sundown.

Mr. W. I believe is "gitting along" pretty well in Detroit, having when he wrote his letter before the last, seven *class* scholars, at six dollars a quarter, each; one private scholar (poor Eddie Larned, who they are afraid is a cripple for life.) for ten dollars a quarter; and three writing scholars at three dollars a quarter. . . . We made out most miserably with our school this winter chiefly through the influence of one bad boy (George Judd) who argued with Mr. Wilson about the pronunciation of the french [sic] word "Fort de quence"; and at another time Mr. Wilson said he wrote a "miserable stick" and then when Mr. Wilson corrected him or rather tried to make him write properly, he said very cooly, "everybuddy's got a way of their own, I han't got your way nor you han't mine." As he was too old for Mr. W. to think of chastising (being a young gentleman of five feet altitude and "stumpy" entirely *out* of proportion) so Mr. Wilson gave him a "talkin' to" and he "got mad" and went off and persuaded all the other "big scholars" to. We had a ball here not long since, and I heard the same young gentleman asking another young gentleman of the same stamp if he had "sent for his pumps yet" to which the aforesaid young gentleman replied that he had not but was "agwine to."[11]

Joseph Kirkland, already interested in dialect at the age of twelve, must have been delighted when he discovered that his mother had included the story of George Judd, disguised as Joshua, in her sketch of the schoolteacher in *Western Clearings* (1845). He was learning to know the people about him in a way which would prove useful to him in the future years when he began to write, and he learned from his mother the habit of carefully recording his observations. He did not, however, have long to spend among the people of Pinckney. Weary of the struggle, in 1843 the Kirklands left the Michigan village to return to New York City.

After eight years in Michigan—two in Detroit and six in the wilderness village of Pinckney—the Kirklands had had their fill of the land fever. They had seen the primeval forest, the refuge of romantic dreams, become an ugly stretch of girdled trees and charred stumps. Their land venture had not been financially successful, and they were ready to return to the East where they might be able to use their knowledge of the West to good purpose.

For the Westerner had taken his place in literature as a type beside the Yankee and the Southerner: the works of writers such as Charles Dickens, Harriet Martineau, and Mrs. Frances Trollope had established him as a singular person. The West had provided material for Caroline Kirkland's writing, and it had given Joseph Kirkland first-hand experience on the frontier among the early settlers of a wilderness village. That experience he could draw upon for his work in *Zury*, for illustrations which would be useful to him in *The McVeys*, and for examples to illustrate points in his histories. It was, as he said, the "beginnings of his 'rustic knowledge' afterwards made use of in his own works."[12]

II *Return to New York*

Joseph Kirkland was thirteen years old when he and his family left Michigan to settle in New York City where his mother had lived in her earlier years and where his parents soon established a school for young ladies in their home at 145 Green Street. Caroline was already a writer of distinction—Poe called her work a sensitive contribution to American literature—and she began writing her third book about western life which she published as *Western Clearings* (1845). Her husband made plans to help the Reverend Dr. H. W. Bellows with his editing of a Unitarian weekly, *The Christian Enquirer;* and to free them for further work, the Kirklands put the youngest son, William, in school in Newburgh, New York. Joseph and his sisters, Elizabeth and Cordelia, remained at home where they studied under their mother's direction.

Their surroundings were happy ones, much more congenial than those of Pinckney had been; and the family interest in literature, education, and religion brought them into contact with a group of writers who were then living in New York. William Cullen Bryant, Horace Greeley, the Duyckinck brothers, Edgar Allan Poe, Anna Mowatt, N. P. Willis—these and others made up the circle in which the Kirklands moved; and Joseph came to know many of the prominent persons with whom his parents associated.

In 1846, when William Kirkland became the editor of the New York *Evening News,* the family not only achieved more prominence but also relief from the financial strain which the venture in Michigan had caused. The future now seemed to hold nothing but happiness. But on October 18, 1846, William, the father, was accidentally drowned; and Caroline had to support the family. Joseph, now sixteen, faced a future in which he had to make his own way.

Caroline turned her entire attention to journalism, gave up the school for girls, and moved her family to 45 Irving Place. She became the editor of the *Union Magazine of Literature and Art* in which she published works of the representative writers of the day: W. C. Bryant, Bayard Taylor, Lydia Maria Child, Catherine Sedgwick, E. A. Poe, Henry D. Thoreau, and others. Her home became also a gathering place of writers; and she made the magazine into a mirror of the times—so successfully that when John Sartain purchased it and moved it to Philadelphia, he retained her in New York as an associate editor.

Joseph, who continued his studies at home, learned French

as a second language and wrote it nearly as well as English. He received the rest of his education informally from his mother's associates; he copied their attitudes and listened to them while longing for means to widen his experience. But when at seventeen he had become shy, his mother decided that he needed the experience afforded by travel. There were a few things which he could do; but—like Melville, who found himself in a similar position earlier—he went to sea: the salt air might be good for him; it might help to fill out his slight figure. So on July 1, 1847, he became a sailor on board a packet plying between England and the United States. He began at once to keep a diary in which he recorded his observations of the ship, his comrades, and the passengers—material which he recalled later when he delineated character in *The McVeys*.

It was not long, however, before his diary was discovered by his comrades who took him to task for his remarks about them. Determined to keep a faithful account of his doings, he wrote the rest of it in French so that the sailors could not read it. Most of the diary was burned in the Chicago fire of 1871, but a few pages in which he recorded his first visit to London were saved. The first entry, dated July 28, 1847, commented about the crossing from the United States:

> Arrived at St. Catherine docks about four o'clock P.M. and kept at work till nearly nine after a voyage of twenty-eight days and a few hours from New York which I left on the first day of July at twelve. I was very seasick for several days without exciting so much merriment among the sailors as I expected. After recovering from *sea* sickness I was brought very low by *home* sickness and was very much comforted by having friends on board. . . . I had a good deal of trouble with my journal on board as the sailors had an idea that I was a spy and managed to get at my book and read what I had written.
>
> I was sick again when I got in the channel on account of the short head sea and my being obliged to keep "watch and watch" which arduous duty I had been excused from before by the kindness of the mate.
>
> We had a very quick passage for the first fourteen days and hoped to make land in sixteen or seventeen days out but were sorely mistaken.[13]

On July 29 he went to visit his Uncle Joseph, Caroline's brother, who had set up a boarding school in London; and at his suggestion, he visited the tunnel of the Thames, Westminster Bridge, the Exchange, St. Paul's, and the Temple Bar. He spent much time writing in his journal and trying to improve his style; but when he visited the British Museum, Longman's in Pasternoster Row, a Jewish "church" and the Tower, he made line sketches of objects which he thought unusual. He went to St. Paul's to church, then to the Zoological Gardens, and the Guildhall. Before long he had exhausted his funds, and he returned to his ship to try to collect some money which he had lent to another sailor. He found his friend penniless, but the two boys decided to make a tour of Greenwich Hospital, Westminster Bridge, and the Poet's Corner in Westminster Abbey. Before long he sailed for Germany, then for a port in France, and thence to the United States, where he landed in the summer of 1848 in time to say good-bye to his mother who was on her way to Europe in the company of Dr. and Mrs. H. W. Bellows.

Kirkland had grown an inch and a half in his year at sea. He was now eighteen years old, and it was time for him to find a job to his liking. Within a short time he had decided on a job in a publishing house, for he aspired to a literary career. In 1852, with his mother's help, he became a clerk and a reader in the offices of *Putnam's Monthly Magazine*.

III *Apprenticeship at Putnam's*

The magazine as well as the office was newly established. Charles F. Briggs—the projector of the magazine who was known to his associates as "Harry Franco"—had edited the *Broadway Journal,* where he had been an associate of Poe. He had gone from that position to the editorship of *Holden's Dollar Magazine,* which had ceased publication in the fall of 1851; in 1852 he approached G. W. Curtis with the idea of a critical magazine. Curtis supported the idea; a publisher, George Palmer Putnam, was found; and the magazine was launched as *Putnam's Monthly Magazine.* The subscription list of the *American Whig Review* was purchased by the editors, and the first number of *Putnam's* was issued in January, 1853. It included work by Henry Wadsworth Long-fellow, James Russell Lowell, and Henry David Thoreau who began his articles on Canada in that issue. Other articles by Horace Greeley, the younger Dana, Fitz-James O'Brien, Herman Melville, and Richard B. Kimball filled other pages.

The second number made a hit with an article by Charles N. Hanson in which he attempted to prove that the Reverend Eleazer Williams was none other than the lost Dauphin of France, a theme later fictionalized by Mary Hartwell Cather-wood in her novel *Lazarre* (1901). In 1854 and 1855 Herman Melville, trying to earn some money by the sale of his work, contributed *Israel Potter* and about half a dozen of his *Piazza Tales.* Cooper's *Old Ironsides,* a sketch of naval his-tory, appeared in the magazine, as did the work of Bayard Taylor, J. P. Kennedy, Charles Dudley Warner, Richard Henry Stoddard, Henry James, and Charles Eliot Norton. Although the magazine was very important and used native materials, it failed in a short time; the *Atlantic Monthly,* which appeared in 1857, used American writers, but did not fail.

Putnam's gave much attention to the West: "We believe in the West,"[14] wrote the editor in the first issue; and Charles Dudley Warner turned out articles about the life of the area, and Parke Godwin, who was political editor, wrote others concerned with the new political movements then beginning to be felt there. Godwin concentrated his interest on the rising Republican Party, which he supported, as did James Russell Lowell; and the articles in *Putnam's Monthly Magazine* called forth from *De Bows* the accusation that it was the "leading review of the Black Republican Party."[15] However, the maga-zine lost its publisher in 1855; but Curtis—who had made some investments in the firm of Dix, Edwards & Company—per-suaded it to become the new publishers in 1856, the year Caroline M. Kirkland's *Study of Washington* appeared in it in serial form.

Joseph Kirkland found the clerkship in the offices of the magazine congenial to his tastes; for, established at a desk in the outer office, he came to know many of the writers of the day, some of whom were also frequent guests at his mother's home. In after years, writing to his daughter Louise Kirkland Sanborn, he recalled one vivid experience of his work in the office of *Putnam's Monthly.* "Dilliwegia," he wrote, using a nickname meaning "Dear Louise":

> I never saw Longfellow that I remember. He was always Boston: we N. Y. He may have been at our house, but I think no. As Bryant adorers and thorough New Yorkers, I think the feeling still dwells in my soul that L. compares with B. as Willis with Irving, or Moore with Byron—diction more elegant, musical, ingenious, artistic; though far less grand and high (Mendelssohn with Beethevon.)
>
> I was a clerk for Putnams' Monthly about 1852 when Longfellow's "Two Angels" came in, in MS. It was (mechanically) a beautiful manuscript; neat, legible, flawless roundhand; every line properly "indented" (It was set forward from the left or kept flush, as its metre might require): in fact ready for the printer—or the photographer in half-tint for that matter —and just such a piece of handwork as one might expect from a poet whose every verse and syllable was made *perfect* before it left his hand—"Genius is an infinite capacity for taking pains." The antipodes of Browning—not to say Walt Whitman who is unspeakable.
>
> I remember carrying it to Mr. Putnam, as much impressed. (It had come anonymously.) Still I thought (and said) that it would have been more ineffably great if two angels, one of life and one of death, had gone hand-in-hand into the chamber of childbirth. Now I don't think so. The other is better.
>
> .   .   .   .
>
> I immediately learned the poem by heart, and I could possibly repeat it today—forty-two years afterward. I have always felt the distinction of having been the *first* among the millions of the public to be struck and awed by the splendid lines. . . .[16]

In the 1850's Kirkland was a dandy about town. Small and elegant and the son of a famous woman writer, Joseph must have been in the heart of the artistic life of the city and a visitor of the theaters: Burton's, the Broadway, the National, Wallack's Lyceum, Niblo's, and Barnum's. He may have seen Fanny Wallack, darling of two continents; Rosa Bennett; and, in *Uncle Tom's Cabin* at Barnum's Broadway Museum, Emily Mestayer fleeing across the river on ice constructed from wood. He certainly met artists and writers: Cranch, Darley, Cole, Ives, Kensett, Powers, Mosier, George Ripley, Griswold —and perhaps Poe and Emerson. Though he always felt more New York than New England, he may have remembered the drowning of Margaret Fuller and her child off Fire Island, and he may have known the saddened Thoreau who came to mourn by the side of the sea. He knew also about the flurry of the Mexican War, the revolution in France, and the discovery of gold in California. And lingering always in his mind were the stories which he had heard about the West.

The covered wagons moved steadily westward, and Kirkland's ideas moved with them. After all, he had already experienced the West; and like his father before him, he had a western fever. Furthermore, as the geographical horizons were pushed back by the western migration, so were the literary horizons. Already the magazines, *Putnam's* not excepted, were not only full of the West but insisted on moving back the curtains to allow for Manifest Destiny and an uncompromising realism. Already the *Spirit of the Times,* Godkin, Godwin, Curtis, Willis, John Charles Fremont, Senator Benton, and thousands of others were insisting on hard facts; and literature was beginning to show characteristics of an uncompromising realism: vulgarity, cruelty, sardonic humor, and violence to which gentle Victorian America closed its eyes, or swept under its ample skirts, or hid under bordered tablecloths. Already there was a beginning of a search for reality—the search which Caroline Kirkland had begun in Michigan.

Joseph Kirkland had somehow to continue the search not only for realism but for El Dorado by moving farther west to raw places. Chicago's sprawling shanties drew him as it did Potter Palmer and Marshall Field, for already that city was the borderland of civilization—the edge of the frontier. Joseph Kirkland itched to be a part of its development; the West was the land of opportunity; there he could stand on his own feet; there he might build the fortune which his father had not been able to make. So he accepted a job traveling as an auditor for the Illinois Central Railroad, and he arrived in Chicago just in time to read about the nomination of John Charles Fremont on the Free Soil Party ticket.

IV   *Early Days in Illinois*

In his new job with the railroad, Joseph Kirkland traveled from Chicago to Cairo at the southern end of the state, and from St. Louis on the western border to Vincennes on the eastern one. He came to know the officials of the road; sometimes he traveled with George B. McClellan, the chief engineer and vice-president. He also met many prominent men of the area, and among them were Judge Davis and his friend Abraham Lincoln, who was already famous because of his debates about slavery with Stephen A. Douglas.

Kirkland's travel also afforded him the chance to observe business opportunities which might be found in the state, for he desired to make more money than he earned with the railroad. In July, 1858, he took a job with the Carbon Coal Company, a mining firm which retailed its product, coal, through Kimball and Company, 109 Lake Street, Chicago. Resigning his position with the Illinois Central Railroad on August 5, he became supervisor of mining operations in the mines at Tilton, Illinois. Tilton and the mines were served by the Great Western Ralroad, and Kirkland found that he could earn additional money by serving as agent for the railroad. He wanted to learn as much as possible about the coal business, mining, transportation, and marketing; for he had already decided that the increasing industrialization of the region around Chicago would bring more and more demands for fuel, and he hoped eventually to enter the coal business as an owner and operator of mines. From his experiences in Tilton and in central Illinois he later drew much of his material for his novels.

In 1858 Tilton was a small village on the banks of the Vermilion River, a few miles from Danville, Illinois, and some seventy-five miles from Springfield, the home of Abraham Lincoln and the capital of the state. Both Tilton and Danville were visited by Lincoln as he traveled the circuit of his law practice, and Kirkland not only knew him but agreed with his political views. Kirkland rose to enough prominence in the ranks of the Republican Party in Illinois to be a member of the committee which waited on Lincoln on May 20, 1860, to inform him of his nomination for the presidency by the Republican Convention in Chicago.

Kirkland's support of Lincoln in his stand against the further extension of slavery was a continuation of family tradition, for William Kirkland, Joseph's father, had been active during his residence in Detroit, Michigan, in helping slaves escape to freedom in Canada. Hatred of slavery, therefore, had been a part of Joseph's heritage; and, when Lincoln was in the White House and the Southern states had rebelled against the Union, Kirkland stood ready to fulfill his duty to his country and his conscience.

During the early part of 1861, however, Joseph Kirkland continued his work as coal mine supervisor for the Carbon Coal Company. He was now thirty years old, and he had varied experiences behind him: the Michigan forests, life in New York, a period at sea, work for one of the more important literary magazines of the time, business experience gained in the auditing division of the Illinois Central Railroad, and jobs as a railroad station agent and as a production manager of coal mines. Although he felt that he could put his knowledge to good use in the coal business, the events of the year interfered with his program for the future—and added to his already varied experiences.

V War Experiences

The election of Abraham Lincoln to the presidency aroused a storm in the South, and the extremists were not long in acting. On December 20, 1860, South Carolina took the lead in secession from the Union. By February 1, 1861, Mississippi, Florida, Alabama, Georgia, Louisiana, and Texas had passed acts of secession. On February 4, 1861, these states formed the Confederate States of America and elected Jefferson Davis as president. Buchanan, then president of the United States, made no move to force the seceding states to remain in the Union; he declared in his message of December 4, 1860, that the Constitution of the United States did not provide the federal government with the power to force a state to remain a member of the Union, but he added that he thought secession unconstitutional. He tried to solve the problem by peaceable means, but in January, 1861, the Confederate batteries on shore off Fort Sumter fired on the *Star of the West,* a federal ship bringing supplies to the fort, and forced her to turn back before she had discharged her cargo. At once the secessionists took charge of the fort in the harbor, the arsenal, and the customhouse at Charleston. At other points in the Confederacy the federal forts and arsenals, with the exception of Fort Pickens at Pensacola, Florida, were taken over by the Southerners. Seventy-year-old President Buchanan refused to take any action. In Illinois, Joseph Kirkland took note of these events and attended meetings in Chicago where the actions of the Southern states had aroused much discussion.

On March 4 Abraham Lincoln became president of the United States; and he chose a cabinet that commanded Northern confidence. In his inaugural address he stressed his responsibility for enforcing the laws of the nation in all parts of an indivisible country. He had hardly entered the White House when word came from Major Anderson, commander at Fort Sumter, that he would have to abandon the fort unless aid came at once. On April 6 Lincoln ordered a relief expedition to the fort; on April 13, after Anderson had refused to surrender, the Confederates opened bombardment, and Anderson surrendered. The loss of Fort Sumter galvanized the North to action. On April 15, 1861, Lincoln issued a call for 170,000 volunteers to serve for three months, and he followed it in May with a request for an additional 42,000 men to serve for three years.

In Illinois Joseph Kirkland volunteered on April 25 for service as a private in Company C, Illinois Twelfth Regiment. To enlist, he went to a great mass meeting in Chicago at the Wigwam, which had been built by the people of the city for the Republican National Convention of 1860. It was a place of action, excitement, and speech-making, for the majority of the prominent persons of the city were in attendance. "The vast plain auditorium of the Wigwam . . . was cloudy with dust and echoing with noise," Kirkland wrote in *The Captain of Company K,* a book written out of "a full heart in memory of his soldier life" in which he recalled many of his own experiences in the Civil War. "Flags, music, speeches, thunders of applause—it seemed as if the Union must be almost saved already. . . . Wit, humor, invective, patriotism, poetry . . . at every pause a fresh cloud of dust arose from the stamping and was blown abroad by the waving of hats and handkerchiefs."

"On long tables in front of the platform were offered eleven subscription papers; ten for signatures of volunteers for Companies A, B, C, D, E, F, G, H, I, and K, and one pledging money for expenses, care of soldiers' families, etc."[17]

Kirkland did not long remain a private in the army. It was the custom of the companies to elect officers, and Company C elected him a lieutenant almost at once. The companies were assembled at Camp Douglas, the rendezvous for Illinois volunteers; at what is now the corner of Cottage Grove and Forest Avenues in Chicago, the camp in 1861 was close enough to the city to allow the soldiers to keep in touch with the happenings there. When Company C was preparing to leave for Cairo, Illinois, Lieutenant Joseph Kirkland, who had provided himself with a uniform, kept busy seeing that his company was supplied with blankets, camp kettles, and other necessities which the citizens of Chicago contributed.

Cairo, situated at the southernmost tip of Illinois and at the confluence of the Ohio and the Mississippi Rivers, was one of the strategic points from which the Union activities could be directed against the South. Memphis, Tennessee, only two hundred miles to the south, could be reached by the Mississippi River; and Nashville, the capital, was only a hundred and thirty-seven miles away. Fort Donelson, on the Cumberland River in Kentucky, could be reached either by the Cumberland, which emptied into the Ohio above Cairo, or by a short overland march. Across the Ohio to the east lay Kentucky; to the south and west, the states of Arkansas and Missouri. Certainly Richard Yates, governor of Illinois, knew the strategic importance of Cairo, and his action in sending troops to that place probably kept the southern part of Illinois from joining the rebellion against the Union; for, since many Southerners had settled in the region, the area was more southern than northern in atmosphere and sympathy.

Kirkland knew the area from his work with Illinois Central Railroad, and he looked forward to his work at the camp which lay north of the cypress swamps which edged Cairo.

But in the camp he found that "toil and drill and study and heat and impatience at what the volunteers thought was unreasonable delay in setting them to work" was the rule of the day. This life tired him rather quickly, and he sought change from it by going into town to the St. Charles Hotel, where he found almost-forgotten luxuries—"a locked door, a glazed window, plastered walls, a half-carpeted floor, a furnished wash-stand, and luxury of luxuries, a mattress bed, with a pillow and bedclothes."[18] He also visited Mound City, Illinois, to see the great army hospital occupying the area which later became a military burial ground; and he went to the naval shipbuilding yards which had grown up in the days of the river traffic. Nestled in a bowl-like space between hills on one side and a sixty-foot levee on the other, Mound City, full of fine old-fashioned houses surrounded by wrought-iron fences, impressed him with its wealth. Since the town teemed with the activity of war, for it was the depot of military supplies for the southern part of Illinois, Kirkland spent much time thinking about changes which war brought to the town. And little by little he came to accept the army life, and he spent considerable time memorizing army regulations.

But Kirkland, as he thought about the war, knew that he could never completely adjust to it. He gradually reached the conclusion that he was not the sort of officer to lead soldiers into battle, and he was soon convinced that he should ask for a transfer to other work. When the gunboat *Aspasia* appeared at Cairo, the Twelfth was loaded on board to be taken down the river to rout the rebels who were gathering in Kentucky; and, after a short skirmish, it returned to Cairo. Kirkland had had a taste of war; it so sickened him that he took advantage of an opportunity to join the staff of his old friend George B. McClellan, who was then in Cairo inspecting the camp. But he had acquired first-hand knowledge which he later used in *The Captain of Company K.*

When the war began, George B. McClellan, a captain in the army under General Winfield Scott in the Mexican War, hastened to organize a company of militia in Ohio, where he was then living. General Scott, to whom he offered his company and his services, secured his appointment to the regular army with the rank of major general and gave him command of territory which included Ohio, Indiana, and Illinois. After he had been appointed early in May, 1861, McClellan began a tour of inspection. He visited Cairo almost at once, and he returned for another visit early in June. He had already found difficulty in securing competent officers, and he may have offered Kirkland a place on his staff during one of these trips. Early in July McClellan entered West Virginia to drive out rebel forces which had gathered there in an attempt to cut the Baltimore and Ohio Railroad. On July 8 the troops were sweltering in the hills and fighting the battle of Laurel Hill. By clearing West Virginia of rebel forces in the following days, McClellan won a reputation which grew as news of his victories spread. On July 22 and after General McDowell had been defeated at the first battle of Bull Run, McClellan was called to Washington by Lincoln and given command of McDowell's forces. On November 1, upon the retirement of General Winfield Scott, McClellan was made general-in-chief of the Union Army.

When he assumed command of McDowell's forces, McClellan began to bring to Washington the staff he had gathered for the West Virginia campaign. Kirkland, hurrying to join his chief, arrived in Washington to serve as an aide-de-camp. On August 26, 1861, he was promoted to the rank of captain. After November 1, when McClellan began the reorganization of the Army of the Potomac, Kirkland served as an aide in the adjutant general's department; and, when the army moved into the field, he was on the personal staff of General McClellan.[19]

During the period of reorganization of the army Kirkland spent much time in Washington. There he came to know John Hay and John Nicolay, secretaries of the President; and, while waiting for orders to be carried to McClellan, he spent many hours telling jokes and talking of the war. He noted that the President spent much time at the great south window of the second story of the White House watching the Union soldiers crossing the bridge to carry the fight into the South. On occasion Lincoln joined the young men to listen to their stories and jokes, and they felt well rewarded for their best efforts when they won a single smile from the care-worn leader.

In the company of Hay and Nicolay, Kirkland moved in the social circles of a city then full of foreign personages. He met the French princes Joinville, Paris, and Chartres, who were members of the general staff and were "perfect gentlemen, but of course just as much and just as little use as officers always are, who instead of climbing up to their places, feel as if they had stepped down into them."[20] He knew as well the correspondent of the London *Times*, delightful old Dr. Russel, a perfect diner-out who was full of stories of the Crimean War but who was a "thorough Tory and disbeliever of our final success, even if we should win all our battles, as he said he thought we should."[21]

Washington was also crowded with business men, bankers, and speculators, many of whom were prominent in their own states. Kirkland met many such men, their wives, and their daughters in the circle in which he moved. Among them was John Wilkinson, a banker from Syracuse, New York, who was also the first president of that part of the New York Central Railroad which ran between Syracuse and Utica. Wilkinson's pretty, vivacious daughter, Theodosia Burr Wilkinson, quickly won the heart of Joseph Kirkland; and he courted her as ardently as he could while helping shape the Army of the Potomac for a campaign in the South. But General McClellan, in spite of loud clamors from the northern press, made no move to lead his troops into battle during the fall of 1861. Christmas and the New Year came and passed, and still McClellan made no move to carry the battle into the Confederacy.

In the meantime the war in the West resulted in Union victories. In February, 1862, General Ulysses S. Grant, headquartered at Cairo in the old Halliday House Hotel, moved against Fort Henry and Fort Donelson near the Kentucky-Tennessee border. The forts surrendered to him in the early weeks of February; and Grant then moved his army on to Nashville, capturing it in his march toward Corinth, Mississippi, the junction of railroad lines from Memphis, Vicksburg, Mobile, and Chattanooga. On April 6 and 7 Grant won the battle of Shiloh and opened the way to the Mississippi River and an approach to the city of Memphis. News of the victories was received with delight by the North. In Washington, General McClellan, recovering from an illness which had kept him inactive in January, prepared to move the Army of the Potomac into Virginia; but he moved so slowly that the campaign did not get under way until April.

On April 21, 1862, the Peninsular Campaign in Virginia finally began. McClellan planned to move his troops by water to the peninsula between the York and the James rivers, but the Confederate frigate *Virginia*—the old United States ship *Merrimac* which the Confederates had clad with iron—threatened the move. McClellan was stopped in his plans; but the Union ironclad *Monitor* appeared, defeated the Confederate ship, and freed McClellan to carry out his campaign. Moving slowly up the country, covering only nine miles from Fortress Monroe to Yorktown in a month, McClellan laid siege to the city. He assigned General Fitz-John Porter, commander of the Fifth Army Corps, the task of taking Yorktown. Kirkland, tired of inactivity, requested a transfer to the staff of General Porter. His request granted, he helped with the siege of the city and with the preparation of headquarters for McClellan after the city had fallen to the Union forces.

McClellan did not follow up the advantage afforded by the capture of Yorktown but continued his slow march toward Richmond. He refused to hurry even after Lincoln, who had held conferences in Washington to obtain the opinion of other military men, had wired him time after time to take advantage of the confusion of the Confederate troops fleeing from Yorktown. Finally Lincoln made a personal visit in May to the headquarters of McClellan; and after much discussion, the writing of many letters, and the sending of many telegrams to and from Washington, McClellan moved toward Richmond. Kirkland, with Fitz-John Porter and the Fifth Army Corps, took part in the battles of Malvern Hill and Hanover Court House. McClellan again halted his forces; but he moved, a month later, toward Richmond once more. At Mechanicsville, Virginia, the Union forces met the Confederates under the command of General Robert E. Lee; and the Union march toward Richmond was stopped by Lee in the battles of Mechanicsville and Gaines's Mill. Two weeks later, at Chickahominy, Lee drove the Union forces back to the James estuary. Kirkland not only took part in these battles but won a commendation for bravery from his commanding general. When

McClellan changed his headquarters from the James River to Harrison's Landing on the New York River, Kirkland became ill there with jaundice and was hospitalized—but not before he was breveted major for his work.[22] His hospital experience provided him with first-hand knowledge for use in his war novel.

While Kirkland was in the hospital, McClellan was recalled by President Lincoln; and General Pope, who had been guarding the city of Washington, was put in command. Pope concentrated his army along Bull Run Creek to face an attack by General Lee; and he ordered General Porter, who was holding the Fifth Army Corps in reserve, to support the center of the line. When Lee attacked the Union forces, which weakened in the center, Pope ordered Porter to march to the support of the line at once; but Porter waited a day before beginning his march. When he arrived at the scene of battle, the Union forces were retreating toward Washington. Pope accused Porter of disobedience because of the latter's loyalty to McClellan, and official reports indicated that the loss of the second battle of Bull Run by the Union forces was brought about by Porter's failure to obey orders. McClellan, placed in command once more, was inclined to support Porter for his action; and the incident was used by his enemies to try to oust him from the army.

Kirkland was discharged from the hospital in time to rejoin Porter's staff before the battle of Antietam, which occurred September 17, 1862, and in which McClellan's forces defeated Lee, who was forced to withdraw from Maryland. In October McClellan was replaced by General Burnside, and in November General Porter was relieved of his command to face court-martial proceedings for "wilful disobedience." In the long trial which followed, the struggle for power in which Secretary of War Stanton, Lincoln's cabinet, and General McClellan were then engaged was clearly revealed.

When Porter was relieved from his post, Kirkland was left inactive; but he volunteered to serve as aide to General Butterfield, who commanded the Fifth Army Corps and who moved his forces to support Burnside in an attack on Lee at Fredericksburg. On December 13 the opposing forces met, and the Union forces were defeated. During the battle, one of the bloodiest of the war, Kirkland had his horse shot from under him. He remained with General Butterfield's staff until January 7, 1863.

When General Porter was cashiered on January 21 and dismissed from the army, his entire staff was reduced one grade in rank and reassigned to McClellan, who had been given an inactive unit. Kirkland, notified of his reduction in rank, decided to resign from the army and return to Tilton to effect his plans to purchase mining lands. On February 22 he requested that the date of his discharge be made January 7, the date on which he had ceased to be actively employed; he stated that his reason for resigning was new responsibilities for his family.

Kirkland left Washington to live with the family of Samuel Stansbury, a brother of his mother who had come to Tilton to open a general store. His war experience had provided him with the raw material for a novel if he could organize it, objectify it, and shape it into fiction which would be a study of war, of men and women during it, and of the social and economic conditions which result from it. But it was to be nearly thirty years before he wrote the novel.

CHAPTER 2

The Struggle Toward Art

W HEN JOSEPH KIRKLAND returned to Tilton, probably in the spring of 1863, he resumed his position as supervisor of mining operations for the Carbon Coal Mining Company, and he became as well the agent for the Great Western Railroad. He was also occupied with the problem of making financial arrangements so that he could purchase enough land to start his own coal mining operations. Although his actual movements can not be accurately traced, he made a trip East sometime during the late fall or early winter of 1863 to visit his mother in New York City and to discuss a career for his brother William, now twenty-four years old. Undoubtedly he came to an understanding with his mother and his brother, and it is more than probable that Joseph suggested a partnership in the coal mining business to William—a theory supported by Louise, one of Kirkland's daughters, who stated that her father had come to some understanding with his brother before he, Joseph, resigned from the army.[1] It is likely that the arrangements may refer to the responsibilities to his family which Joseph Kirkland gave as his reason for resigning his commission.[2] Whatever his plans may have been, they were sufficient to allow him to persuade Theodosia Burr Wilkinson to become his wife; they were married on December 29, 1863.

Joseph Kirkland's father-in-law, John Wilkinson, was a man of considerable wealth and a speculator in railroads. In the period of railroad expansion which preceded the Civil War, he had made a comfortable fortune as the first president of the New York Central Railroad; and he was interested in investments in the new railroads which were then being projected for the West as a result of the Congressional charters of the Union Pacific and Central Pacific railroads, which had been granted in 1862. Wilkinson acquired in Joseph Kirkland a son-in-law whose plans for his own business expansion in the West followed a pattern much to the liking of an Eastern railroad man who realized the importance of coal mining for railroads which were to extend across the continent. Joseph Kirkland acquired a father-in-law who was wise in the ways of the business world, who was a fountain of advice, and who was also a source of finance to be tapped for pursuance of Kirkland's plans in Illinois. Kirkland learned enough about railroading from him to use the information in *The McVeys.*

Joseph and Theodosia Kirkland made the trip from Syracuse to Tilton in the first month of 1864. The winter was unusually cold; and, as the slow train moved westward, Theodosia saw prairie states for the first time. She could hardly believe her eyes as she viewed the hardships of western life in the midst of a winter which Kirkland in *Zury* referred to as "eighteen-hundred-and-froze-to-death!" Chickens were frozen to the trees in which they had roosted, and cattle lay frozen in heaps in the barnyards and fields. The life which lay ahead of Theodosia was new and hard for a city-bred girl, but at once she set about making adjustments to her new surroundings in the raw village of Tilton and planning a home for which she had brought many things from Syracuse.

The newly married couple stayed with Samuel Stansbury and his family until they could rent a big, old-fashioned house on the Tilton-Danville road. Settled in the house, Theodosia began to worry about her belongings, and especially about the silver family heirlooms brought with her as wedding gifts from her father and mother. Fearful that some of the neighbors, who seemed rough and somewhat lax in morals to the young bride, would make away with her silver, Theodosia made a trap door in a closet in the floor and hid it; she was unaware that all passers-by could view it from the road.

While Theodosia worried about her heirlooms, Joseph spent much time at the mines, directing the digging of coal out of the shallow shafts and seeking lands which would be suitable for his projected venture as an independent operator. Before he had found desirable land for purchase, however, he was called to New York by the sudden death of his mother, who had succumbed to apoplexy brought on by overwork in her attempts to aid the Union cause by helping Dr. H. W. Bellows, who had organized the United States Sanitary Commission, to raise money to provide food and supplies for Union soldiers and their families; to do so, she had managed one of the departments of a great exhibition.[3]

Joseph was grief-stricken; he had always been close to his mother, had followed her advice in matters of education and work, and had been happy because of her success and fame. After her death he had to assume responsibility for Elizabeth and Cordelia, his two sisters, and for William, his brother. Caroline had been the guiding spirit of their lives; without her and incapable of planning, they depended upon Joseph to arrange matters for them. At once Joseph decided that his sisters and brother should return to Tilton with him. Gathering their mother's manuscripts, the portrait of their father which Caroline had long cherished, their books, household goods and personal belongings, the four children of Caroline Kirkland departed for Illinois.[4]

I *The Prairie Chicken*

Settled in Joseph's home in Tilton, the Kirkland children discussed plans for continuing the work which their mother had begun for the United States Sanitary Commission; but they could hardly raise money by a fair in Tilton, for the town was too small to support such an enterprise. In the search for methods of raising funds, they hit upon the idea of publishing a paper which they decided to call *The Prairie Chicken* because the name suggested something "rich, spicy, popular and wholesome."[5] The income from the paper was to be given to the Sanitary Commission; the price to subscribers requiring delivery by mail service was one dollar a year; but local subscribers, calling at the office for the paper, might have it for fifty cents a year. The place of issue was Tilton, but the printing was done by D. S. Crandall, editor of the *Champaign County Union;* J. George Day of Chicago donated the paper for the publication.[6]

Subscriptions to the paper came from all parts of the country; the paper found its way to places as widely separated as San Francisco and Boston where the *Transcript* once mentioned it by name.[7] By December, 1864, the Kirklands were able to send a check to the Treasurer of the Sanitary Commission; and by September 1, 1865, when the editors summarized the work in which they had been engaged, they had raised four hundred dollars for the organization.

Although the Kirklands desired to raise money, they were also eager to make sure that the village of Tilton, "our new community should be represented in the periodical literature of the nation, though ever so humbly, thus encouraging our fellow citizens to feel that there is no path of advancement shut out from us if we will avail ourselves of every opportunity of improvement."[8] The Kirklands knew many of the writers of the East, and one of them, Lydia Maria Child, submitted "God Bless Our Soldier Boys" for publication. The poem was accepted and appeared in the November 1, 1864, issue. The paper, which was published from October 1, 1864, to September 1, 1865, did not name the editor; but there is little doubt that Joseph Kirkland guided the project or that his sister Elizabeth did the major portion of the editorial work.

II *Experiments in Writing*

Joseph Kirkland probably did his first serious writing for the paper, for it presented an opportunity for him to record for publication ideas he had long been forming. In the first issue he published "The Visit," a piece of doggerel. Of more interest, however, is a series called "Moral Perspectives" in which he tried to point to real values in living and in which he compared a man who devotes his life to piling up money to one who loads himself with stones until the pile on his back is so heavy that he at last succumbs to the burden which determined by the shift of the weight his path in life. Later, he castigated the assumed elegance of ladies who adopted an entirely superior attitude toward servants, and he also pointed to the moral obligation which each person had to aid all less fortunate than he.

His publications also indicate that, although Kirkland had resigned his commission, he maintained his interest in the

Civil War and the consequences of the conflict. Believing in the righteousness of the Union cause, he wrote in "God's Country" that the very idea implied in the use of such words reflected the American idea that the United States was a favored land. Pointing to the selfish motives of men, he suggested that the country could remain a favored spot only if each person maintained a "wish for the best and highest good of all God's creatures."[10]

In another article in which he mulled over the features of the rebellion, he wrote:

> There is a point respecting this unholy rebellion which seems to have been passed over far too lightly. Those who lived in the days of sturdy old Andrew Jackson will remember well how much it injured the Whigs of that time to be even suspected of the least sympathy with the British, so that the term "British Whig" did more to overthrow the Whigs than anything else. Why was this? Was it not because our people cherished a deep and wholesome jealousy of all monarchial government, and regarded him as no better than a traitor to his country and to liberty who thought of enlisting the aristocrats of the Old World in any of our American quarrels? . . . Nothing so clearly marks the decay of public virtue as the willingness to gratify hatred against our brethern by calling in outsiders. . . .

He then pointed out that the southern leaders, by sending Slidell and Mason to Europe to secure aid to "crush out our liberties and establish Slavery and Aristocracy," had violated American tradition and had shown that civilization in the South had decayed.[11]

Kirkland then speculated about the length of time a truly representative government might exist in the United States; he cited the facts that the character of the citizenry had changed and that personal interest had replaced public interest in the minds of many as possible proof that men no longer desired a government of the type devised "with consummate wisdom, arranged with laborious thoroughness, prompted and ennobled by rare faith in human nature." He also thought that party machinery had not entirely taken the place of an honorable public spirit; and he asserted that the moral tone of the nation had become so lowered that men possessing no talent were able to get themselves elected as representatives of the people. He believed that the best men were then serving in the army while less talented ones tried to run the government and direct their actions. He then suggested that the moral tone of the government had been weakened by the liberal treatment of foreigners who not only had little comprehension of the form of American government but deliberately sought to bring about its downfall. The only hope for the government and the only manner of reducing the rebellion, he concluded, lay in a purification of our decadent morals and in a return to the principles upon which the founding fathers had acted.[12]

In the issue for May, 1865, he regarded the defeat of the Confederate States as the fall of one of the "grandest and most nefarious schemes of a national destruction and construction the world ever saw." He was overjoyed to know that the war had ended, but his happiness turned to grief when Abraham Lincoln's assassination "fell like a pall on the National joy. . . . Our joy is turned to mourning. . . . As for the dead, he needs no tears. He stood so high in honor that there was only one rank above his—that of our hero martyrs; and now to that rank he has been promoted. There was one depth not yet sounded by Rebel degradation. To that depth it has now fallen. . . ."[13]

In June, 1865, Kirkland turned his attention to the problem of reconstruction which occupied the entire nation. By then a group of radicals in the Republican party were already attempting to reduce the South to the status of an enslaved state, and Kirkland advised against such violence. The reduction of the South to submission was no reason to continue the punishment, he thought. "Justice demands punishment—never revenge," he wrote; and he also pointed out that the South had suffered greatly: "Her lands are desolate, her granaries are empty; her women are weeping in sables, her slaves are free men, her pride is broken. . . ." He then posed his solution:

Now, to raise this prostrate foe, who, we must not forget it, has fought us most valiantly, to bind his wounds and build up his strength with care is a harder demand upon the talent of Government than it was to break him to the ground, as the work of a creator is always greater than that of a destroyer.

The day for Jackson severity has gone by. Had Mr. Buchanan the quality, we should not now see so many maimed men and weeping women; but at this time wisdom and moderation—justice, but justice tempered with mercy—should be the guides of the administration.[14]

Because his statement clearly demonstrated his personal feelings concerning reconstruction, Kirkland turned his attention to other matters. The possibility of a financial crash which he thought could follow the war particularly concerned him; and he had written as early as March, 1865, that persons who speculated in American goods during war were traitors to their country—a point he later made in his descriptions of mercantile Chicago in his war novel. Furthermore, he pointed out that such action must eventually cause a financial crisis in the manufacturing circles of America; and by May, 1865, he foresaw a depression: "The great public might as well be taught to comprehend, first as last, that the so-long anticipated revulsion in the monetary affairs of this country is, in all probability, close at hand." He then added a warning and an explanation:

The natural result of a civil war is, of course, an enormous increase of the national expense. To meet this increase there must be a proportionate augmentation of government indebtedness involving, as it has done with us, a vast expansion of the volume of paper currency. This expansion inflates prices. Prices thus inflated are bubbles, and bubbles only. They have not substance in them, and there is no solidity in the glitter of their apparent prosperity. The first peace prospect—the first clear evidence of a return to regular business times and a specie basis—pricks this bubble, and it collapses with a gush. That collapse is now momentarily expected. . . . The price of peace, after years of warfare, is the temporary but complete overthrow of commercial credit; the exhaustion of our business resources; the abject prostration of values and the uttter disorganization of all the elements of trade. The payment of this price means the bankruptcy of three-fourths the merchants, great and small, throughout the land. . . .[15]

In another article in the same issue of May, 1865, he pointed to the speculators in gold, "merchandise, and all the necessaries of life, who have so long forestalled the markets and shaved the consuming millions"; who "bellow"; and whose "newspaper organs depreciate a swift return to specie payments, lest the gamblers should be utterly smashed." Kirkland thought that such speculators deserved to be smashed completely, and he voiced the hope that they would lose everything which they had made from speculative ventures.

Living as he had for some time in Illinois, Kirkland was aware that the agricultural interests of America must suffer during times of financial panic. Corn, he thought was the "gold dust of the prairies," the "manna of the treeless wilderness," and "the sunshine of the frontiersman." Out of it came the "beef, pork, whiskey, clothing, houses, comfort, wealth, travel, art, literature, life and love, all in the original packages"; but, although financial reverses were felt by farmers during depressions, Kirkland was certain that they were better off than city people who had no means of producing their own food. The farmer might not have money, but he rarely went hungry.[16] Kirkland had begun to form an idea of farm life which he could use for creating fiction when he had the time to write it.

Kirkland's article on corn and its relation to the finance of agricultural areas provided him with an opportunity to comment about the effect which the cultivation of the crop had on the life of farmers. He noted that "corn has a nomenclature of its own as well as an empire. . . . People are born, marry, and die, about 'plantin' time,' 'roas'-near' time, &c, &c,." Explaining his statement more fully, he wrote:

Plantin' time is early May. Firs' plowin' is early June. "Laying by" . . . is simply the season when the corn has been plowed often enough to overpower the weeds, and so take care of itself. Then it is "turned out" like cattle in the woods, or "laid by" when the man, plowing his field till sundown, has to stand on his horse to see his way home over the corn tassels. Corn "in the silk" and "in the milk" or "jest a makin'" are in August.—Then comes the most important epoch, "Roas' nears."

He also pointed out that there was a difference between "eastern, or retail culture" and that of the West where corn was grown in abundance. In the East, he said, corn hoeing or husking bees were social affairs; but in the prairie sections of Illinois such practices were unknown.

Kirkland later used the material in this article about corn in his first novel, *Zury: The Meanest Man in Spring County*, to give local color and reality to the setting.[17] He employed his observations for his articles in the paper, and these later formed the setting for his characters, the episodes, and the realities of his fictional studies.

During the period when he was writing for *The Prairie Chicken*, he was working as a supervisor of mining operations; and this work supplied material for a series of articles which appeared in February, March, and June, 1865. In the first article he dwelt upon the bounteous qualities of a nature which had supplied coal for consumption by a native people. He asserted that coal had helped to win the recent war by enabling railroads to function properly; and he added that coal mines had contributed to the general welfare of the nation, for coal operators paid a tax of five cents a ton on the coal produced. He also speculated about the possibility that coal might be a good fertilizer because he had observed that hogs seemed to like it; he thought that, if it were good for animal tissue, it ought to be good for vegetable tissue. Even the smoke from passing trains might serve to help the growth of vegetation.

In his second article he described the proper terminology to use in speaking of coal mining, explained the processes of mining, and ended with the problem of the operator's being caught between the consumer and the producer even as a "grain of wheat between the upper and nether millstone." This last thought was an introduction to the material which he included in his third and last article in which he presented his ideas about the formation of unions by coal miners.

The formation of labor unions, Kirkland felt, was a deliberate attempt to destroy normal prices by actions which suspended the laws of supply and demand. He declared that joining a union was an act of perverse and warped judgment, an example of unreliable human nature. "All nature is reliable except Human nature," he insisted, "and that is unaccountable, unfathomable in its currents and counter-currents, unstable and illogical, inconsistent, impracticable—everything, in fact, that begins with *un,* or *il,* or *in,* or *im.*"

After comparing the vagaries of human nature with the stable qualities of coal, he introduced his ideas about labor. The man who didn't pay his men enough soon lost them to someone else; the man who didn't do enough work to earn his pay soon lost his job; but, Kirkland said, the coal miners combined to overrule these normal reactions. They formed a "trade union" with the intent of regulating affairs according to their own ideas. He felt that their ideas were not good ones in spite of the arguments which the union men presented—that all would benefit from the unions. Furthermore, he did not like to think that men would join the union because of the argument that no man had a right to overwork himself. He felt that the union argument that no man had the right to overstock the market was not valid, and he was certain that the union would sooner or later use force to get members. He knew that the operators did not like the idea of a union; and, though some companies would be successful in opposing it for a short time, he believed that such opposition would not be effective until "hard times" forced men to seek employment, "instead of vice versa." When such times came, men would have all they could do to support their families without spending their money needlessly on "miner unions."

In the last issue of the paper of September, 1865, Kirkland commented about an editorial supporting labor unions which he reprinted from the New York *Evening Post*: "We noticed sometime since that the *Post* was devoting its space and influence to the encouragement of the gigantic 'Workingmen's Union' which certain persons (probably not working men) are trying to establish. Strange, that a paper which so consistently and so ably advocates free foreign trade, should countenance fettered domestic trades?" He then asserted that the movement was vicious, and he was convinced that arguments in its favor were specious: "First, on abstract principles, applying the analogies which are suggested by the old well-known laws of trade. . . . Second, by the light of experience

as furnished by the history of other 'protective efforts.' . . .
Third, by allowing the combiners to go ahead—try their experience once more, forcing all workmen into their association
and all employers into their system, until it topples down by
reason of its foundations having been laid in the shifting sands
of false political economy." He felt that all unions were the
work of .men who "always think wages too low, hours too
long, work too hard, . . . and the 'Rights of Man,' generally,
abused by 'Capital.' "

Kirkland had formed an opinion of labor unions which he
never changed. By nature, by training, and by marriage, he
was aligned with the employer class; and he had little patience
with those who held opinions different from his own. Having
made his pronouncements about unions in *The Prairie Chick-
en,* he moved to another problem which was paramount in the
interests of persons of his era: the railroads.

Since his first arrival in the West in 1856, Kirkland had
been associated with railroads. His work with the Illinois
Central had provided his livelihood until he found a better
job; he had served as an agent for the Great Western for
some years; and his wife was the daughter of a railroad execu-
tive. Moreover, if he entered the coal mining business for
himself, the railroads would be potential customers. Because
of these facts, it is not odd that Kirkland defended the
railroads from the charges of restraint of trade which were
then being brought against them—a charge which was to
culminate in the rise of the agrarian West in an attempt to
control the network of lines which gradually spread over the
nation.

The first of his articles in defense of the roads appeared in
April 1865; entitled "The Illinois Central Railroad," the article pointed out that, although the company had received
two and a half million acres of land from the government,
it had enabled the government to retrieve whatever the land
had been worth. Since only alternate sections of land had
been given to the railroad and since the price of the inter-
vening sections had been raised by the government from one
dollar and a quarter an acre to two dollars and fifty cents
an acre—an increase possible only because the land lay along
a railroad—the government had realized as much from half the

land as it could otherwise have received for the total acreage. Furthermore, he said, the government had the best of the deal, for the stock which had cost one hundred dollars a share in gold when the company was first formed had declined to sixty dollars. The loss of interest by the company while it struggled to hold its own through hard times increased its total losses, and any person ought to be able to see that the company had invested twice as much as its present market value.

Kirkland also noted that the charter for the company had originally provided that the railroad "shall be a free highway for the transportation of Government property and troops, forever." Such an arrangement during the Civil War would have ruined the road! The government, aware that the railroads could not bear the extra cost alone, had decided that the term "public highway" meant that the company provided the road but the government could run over that road any vehicles it might possess. If the government owned no vehicles, Kirkland argued, it was only reasonable that the company should be paid for the actual cost of operation of its own vehicles when they were operated entirely for the convenience of the government. The rate of pay, he thought, was within reason since it was two-thirds the rate which the government paid to roads holding charters in which "land-grant clauses" did not appear. But, he declared, the roads lost money by the arrangement with the government. Increased business during the war made possible the payment of higher rates by private enterprise. The road could, therefore, have raised its rates and made much more money than it could possibly clear by any other method. When he observed that many persons thought that railroads should be owned and operated by the government, he asserted that such persons were naive, for they knew nothing about the inefficiency of government in business. Closing his article with the statement that many people thought the railroads were merely huge monopolies supported by the government, Kirkland declared that his statements sufficiently refuted such ideas.

In his second article about railroads in *The Prairie Chicken* of April, 1865, Kirkland tried to be more literary. The essay was concerned with the progress, luxury, and convenience in travel which the roads made possible. He pointed to time-saving factors, the luxury of sleeping cars, the rapidity with which produce was carried from the farm to the city market, and the close relationship between the different sections of the country brought about by the railroads. He thought that if by 1875 the roads were able to maintain a speed of seventy-five miles an hour—as did the English railroads of the time—New York would then be nearer than Ohio was at the time of his writing. Giving his imagination free play, he foresaw a possible speed of one hundred and forty miles an hour, larger cars, improvements such as the compound steel-capped rail, and the immense saving of time which would result. "To save a day, each, for ten thousand people is equivalent to saving almost a lifetime for one man," he wrote, impressed by his own figures. He had completed his defense of the railroads.

Not all of Kirkland's writing for *The Prairie Chicken* dealt, however, with problems of economics or government, for he tried his hand at purely literary pieces. In March, 1865, he published a sketch in dramatic form. Centering the locale in rebel territory, he tried to use the appropriate dialect to convey an idea of his characters, a girl of thirteen and her grandmother. The women were "denizens of the piney wood" of the region near the Pearl River in Mississippi. The work, clearly that of an amateur, was his first attempt to simulate reality in handling dialogue.

In another sketch, "A School Exhibition Piece," published in the issue of March, 1865, he tried to use dialect to show the difference between Confederate and Union soldiers. He also explained the difference in morals by having the Rebel declare his willingness to be friendly with any person who could supply him with whiskey and by portraying the Union soldier's disgust about the Rebel's lack of responsibility. In the final scene, symbolizing the defeat of the Confederacy, the Union soldier captures the Rebel. An amateurish piece, it provided Kirkland with further practice in writing dialogue.

In a third sketch of April, 1865, based on the reading by two army officers of Tennyson's *Enoch Arden*, Kirkland indicated that he thought that most officers had little learning and less culture. The short sketch closes abruptly when the junior officer notices that his superior has fallen asleep from boredom.

In a sketch published in the issue for July, 1865, Kirkland, writing about his acquaintance with Lincoln, recalled a visit of the great man to Tilton and some other occasions when he had seen the martyred president. He remembered that he had always been impressed with the air of suffering which Lincoln seemed somehow to convey, and he felt that Lincoln had always known that his own fate was involved in the affairs of the nation. Kirkland realized that Lincoln had held unswervingly to one purpose and that, when opportunities came for accomplishment, he had seized them unhesitatingly only to become doubtful afterwards. Lincoln was, Kirkland thought, the one man he had known who was constantly aware of the tragic character of life, and his death was a blow to Kirkland who felt that national affairs were ably and humanely directed by the president.

Among the articles which appeared in *The Prairie Chicken* were three essays by Caroline Matilda Kirkland, "taken from unpublished MSS. . . ."[21] The first is a fragment about the virtues of country life as compared to city life; the second, an essay about concerts; and the third, an essay about works of fiction "written as a preface to an unpublished novel" in which Mrs. Kirkland pointed out that the joy which a reader gains from a novel results from a catharsis of emotion. Because readers imagine real characters, she wrote, it is the duty of the novelist to teach morals by drawing characters as nearly real as possible; and a writer who is unfaithful to reality is more dangerous than "unveiled evil." She believed that society in America was increasingly disposed to luxury and wealth; it had forgotten the simple and frugal habits of earlier men. These habits, she thought, must be cultivated in children if republican maxims of government were to exist in the minds of the people of the United States. Her aim was to write simple history to illustrate the virtues supporting a sound society, and her son Joseph adopted her principles in his own fiction.

Caroline Kirkland's essays were included in the paper to form a sort of monument to the work which she had started for the benefit of the United States Sanitary Commission. No doubt her children were impressed also by her writing; for Joseph was already trying to write in a manner which would reproduce incident and character "pentagraphed from reality." He had not yet succeeded because he needed more time in which to write; but his practice pieces in *The Prairie Chicken*, though rough and unfinished, were the beginnings of ideas which he could not forever delay expressing. This work also reveals that he was a keen observer who paid attention to character and dialect; but these habits were not new to him: he had cultivated them since his early boyhood in Michigan.

Kirkland desired to write, but he had no time. First he had to establish himself financially, and this struggle occupied his attention for the next twenty years. After achieving financial security, he thought he would write a novel which would follow his mother's pattern by presenting life in all its reality. But with the last issue of *The Prairie Chicken* in 1865 Joseph Kirkland interrupted his writing career to turn his attention to the acquisition of coal lands. He did not begin to write again until after the Chicago fire of 1871.

III *Operator of Coal Mines*

In the years immediately after the Civil War Kirkland devoted his attention to business problems. In a period of general expansion, Illinois felt the effects almost at once. Situated in a favorable position for transportation by lake and by rail, Chicago entered a period of unprecedented growth; and shortly a high proportion of all the manufacturing industries of the state was situated within that city or its environs.[22] The city was the terminus for all the more important railroad lines stretching to the Atlantic, the Pacific, the Gulf of Mexico, and the Northwest; and, because local roads were constructed to carry the fuel necessary for the expansion of business, Illinois had the greatest railroad mileage of any state in the Union.[23] The localization of industry in the northern and central counties of the state was made possible, therefore, by the improvement of transportation facilities; and the commercial interests in grain, flour, livestock, provisions, lumber, wool and hides, seeds, and coal were centered there.

In Tilton, Illinois, Joseph Kirkland decided it was time to enter business for himself. He made arrangements with his brother William to become his partner; and in November, 1865, the two of them purchased land in the region of Grape Creek, four miles south of Tilton.[25] The land—rough, hilly, and undeveloped—had veins of coal which lay close to the surface and which outcropped in many places; the two brothers planned, therefore, merely to scrape away the earth to mine the coal. Joseph used his connections with the railroads to secure a contract with the Illinois Railway Company (now the Chicago and Eastern Illinois), which agreed to buy all the coal the Kirkland mines could produce.[26] The mines did well from the beginning; and in the spring of 1866 Joseph bought two adjoining lots in Danville, Illinois, evidently with the aim of building a house. At the same time William purchased the house in which the family then lived.[27]

Joseph used his time to consolidate his business, to establish new contacts, and to try to increase the production of the mines. He had talked with some of the miners who had come from Belgium, and they told him of the method of production of coal in that country where, because of the depth of the mines and the limited quantities of coal deposits, the operators had learned to process their product to assure high quality and at the same time to use conservation methods which were necessary if the mines were to operate over a long period of years.

Stimulated by his interest in the Belgian methods and feeling financially secure, Kirkland planned a European trip with his family. Caroline, his eldest daughter, born on March 20, 1865, and baby Louise, born on November 7, 1866, were young enough to be little trouble; and Joseph felt that he should visit Europe with his wife before their family grew to such proportions that parental duties would keep them from travel. Accordingly the family sailed from New York early in the spring of 1867.

Joseph planned to visit England first to see his uncle, Joseph Stansbury. Then the family would go to Germany, a nation then becoming an industrial country, where Joseph felt that he might learn something about mining. George Bancroft, whom Kirkland's father had known in student days at Göttingen, was the newly appointed minister to Berlin who could provide means by which Joseph could inspect the mines of Germany.[28] Finally, the family had to visit Belgium and particularly the mining areas of the Ardennes, where Joseph could learn the process of making coal into bricks by soaking it in water and pressing it while it was wet. If he could make the same sort of bricks in Illinois, he might be able to supply the newly established iron factories with a product which would make it possible for them to employ new processes already used in the East to produce steel.

No actual record of the trip is extant, but the Kirklands returned to Tilton in the fall of 1867. Joseph began to try the Belgian method of making bricks of coal. He brought machinery, a watering trough in which to soak the coal, and a machine to press out bricks. He did not stop his regular production of coal, for he knew that he was experimenting; he hoped to make money by the new process and to be a leader in coal conservation. Industrial leaders of the state were not interested, however, in the process; there was far too much coal for them to be concerned with the problem of conservation. And Joseph Kirkland soon found that his investment would not pay off.

Having spent much time and money in the experiment, he now turned his entire attention to the marketing of coal and he determined to form a retail outlet in Chicago. His brother could handle most of the details of mining the coal, and he could stimulate sales in Chicago. Assuming that he would be able to carry out his plans, he decided to move his family to Chicago where larger cultural interests would afford opportunities for them to participate in projects which were not possible in a small town.

IV   *Removal to Chicago*

In 1868 Kirkland moved his family to a rented house on Huron Street in Chicago. Located three doors west of Cass Street, the home was, therefore, conveniently near the business district. By the middle of the summer the family was settled; and on October 22, 1868, Theodosia Kirkland gave birth to a son, who was named John Wilkinson Kirkland in honor of his maternal grandfather. Joseph rented space for a coal yard on Lake Street, and he began to establish his business. Elizabeth and Cordelia, his two sisters, decided to move to the city, and they took a house on Dearborn Street. Trained as they had been by Caroline Kirkland to be useful, the two sisters decided to supplement their slender income from property left to them by their mother; and, following the example of their parents, they established a school for young ladies in their Dearborn Street house. The coal yard and the school did well, and the Kirkland family in Chicago settled down to life in a rapidly growing city.

Becoming members of the fashionable Unitarian congregation of Unity Church, they developed a close friendship with the minister, the Reverend Robert Collyer. Collyer was a well-known civic leader; and, as he and Joseph became closer friends, he influenced Joseph to become interested in the growth and cultural development of the city. Joseph remembered Old Fort Dearborn, "with its picturesque over-hanging upper story, built in that shape in order that it might be better defended from the torch of the Indian," which he had seen standing "lonely and deserted on the river bank" when he had first come to Chicago in 1856.[29] He wanted to know more about the settlement of the city, and he dreamed of writing a history when he had the time. He could find little time during this period, however, because his Chicago coal business demanded his attention, and he had to make regular trips to Tilton to advise his brother about the production of the mines. But he looked forward to the future contentedly; he believed that his business would soon make him financially secure. But again, disaster overtook him.

By the summer of 1871 the rapid growth of Chicago had given the city a total of 56,000 buildings, most of them built of pine. Because of its location, the city was exposed to strong sweeping winds which passed over the flimsy frame buildings. The summer of 1871 was a dry one, the whole country suffered from severe drought, and in Chicago almost no rain fell during the summer months. But the summer passed, October came, and on Sunday, October 8, Joseph Kirkland took the train to Tilton for one of his regular inspection trips. During the night a fire started in the western part of the city, where severe damage had been done by fire the previous day. The populace felt no general alarm, for the river was considered sufficient protection for the north and south divisions of the city. But the fire was accompanied by a fierce dry wind which, like a gigantic blowpipe, drove the blaze before it; and by Monday night most of the city lay in ruins.[30]

The Kirklands had spent Sunday, October 8, in their usual way, "some of us going over the scene of the West Side fire of the night before and espying from a good distance, the unhappy losers of so much property. . . ." Cordelia Kirkland wrote to cousins in Utica, New York,[31] that by ten o'clock in the evening the firebells rang continuously and that by midnight the fire had crossed the river. The entire city seemed to be on fire; Cordelia and her sister Elizabeth gathered together a few articles and fled from their home. The whole city was aroused; people dashed in terror in all directions, shouting, screaming, and cursing. Bits of burning wood were carried by the wind, and new fires started from them. The whole atmosphere of the city was unreal—a nightmare which the people of Chicago could hardly believe.

In Tilton, Joseph Kirkland heard the news of the great fire and hurried back to the city where he arrived at daylight on Tuesday, October 10.[32] His wife had been awakened by the fire shortly after midnight, and her brother Dudley, who lived nearby, had tried to calm her fears. But she had dressed the children and had sent them north in her brother's carriage while she remained behind to save some belongings. She sent a message to the nearby livery stable for her own pony phaeton. She packed the family silver and a few garments, tied them into a bundle in a sheet, and drove to the place where her children were already lodged. But by six in the morning they were forced to leave their temporary haven. In the pony phaeton they fled still farther northward into the section beyond Lincoln Park.

Joseph was unable to believe that destruction could be as bad as rumored, but when he saw hundreds of people carrying buckets, pitchers, barrels, and casks to the lake to get water he suspected that the rumors were true. His train could not get to the Twelfth Street Station, so he had to walk from Twenty-second Street. All about him was ruin—State

Street was obstructed with bent streetcar rails, and the buildings were empty shells. The clear autumn morning made the contrast greater; the early morning sun shone on blackened remains of a city. Joseph turned to his own home to find the house burned, the distorted remains of its contents still blazing in the cellar. He knew that his wife and children must be safe, and he set out to find them. He hired a farmer to drive him northward; before long, he had joined his family.[33]

The family was together again, but it was homeless, and Joseph had suffered severe business losses. His coal yard had burned; he had no insurance;[34] and he had to find a place for his family to live. There was only one thing to do: his wife and children must go East to her father in Syracuse until he could provide a place for them. Sending them there, he stayed in Chicago to face the task of rebuilding.

The total area of the burned district covered over two thousand acres; 13,500 buildings had been consumed; and nearly a hundred thousand people were homeless. The financial loss reached nearly $188,000,000, and individual fortunes suffered greatly. About $90,000,000 of the loss had been insured, but not more than $40,000,000 of it was collectible. The major insurance companies began to pay at once, but some of the smaller ones were forced to suspend payment because they could not meet the great losses which they had incurred. The outlook for the people of Chicago was dark, but the Liverpool, London, and Globe Insurance Company announced that it would pay three million dollars of the loss at once.[35]

The result was electric. Bankers met to discuss plans for rebuilding the city; lumber dealers announced that they would keep the price of lumber down; and the city began Phoenix-like to rise from its ashes. Kirkland bought a lot in his wife's name; in her name also he let contracts for a four-story house; and, when it was finished in 1873, he recorded the deed in her name alone. The lot was on the corner of Rush and Superior streets. Not far away at 135 Rush Street, Cyrus McCormick built his house, and the fashionable Marquette and Victoria apartment houses stood but a short distance away. On April 19, 1874, Theodosia Kirkland gave birth to another daughter, Ethel, the last of the four Kirkland children.

Soon the Kirkland house became the popular gathering spot for the children of the neighborhood.

Joseph was still in difficult financial circumstances, and he had not cleared himself of debt when the panic of 1873 hit the country. The inflated currency and credit of the years following the Civil War had allowed millions of dollars to pour into the factories and mills of the United States, and production far outstripped demand. Furthermore, the construction of railroads had been so great that almost a billion dollars had been invested in them; and indebtedness had piled up until it was impossible to pay it off. Much of the expansion had been financed from European sources, and dishonesty played a part in much speculation. In May, 1873, a panic in Vienna, which spread to other capitals of Europe, caused withdrawals of a great part of the support of American business. American bankers were unable to assume the additional load, and the country headed for a depression.

The crash came in September when the failure of the company of Jay Cooke, which had financed the Northern Pacific Railroad, plunged the financial world into fear and excitement. Banks and clearinghouses closed; railroads defaulted on their bonds; industrial activities ceased; and more than three million wage-earners were out of jobs. In the West the farmers, who had mortgaged their holdings to acquire new lands or to invest in newly developed machinery, found their grain a drug on the market; and they were without means to meet their mortgage payments.

In Illinois, the farmers banded together to fight the evils which they felt resulted from the credit system of Wall Street. Elaborately organized with all the appeal of secrecy and ritual, the Grange movement grew rapidly and began to have real force. The first Grange had been organized in the office of *The Prairie Farmer* in Chicago in 1868, and now Granges became widespread;[36] as the movement developed, it formed a political group which later was known as the Populists. The economic unrest of the West found in the currency question a specific object to shoot at in a political battle, for laborers and farmers began to view with disfavor the policy of retiring or funding paper money not backed by specie in favor of long-term bonds. The western debt had been accumulated in greenbacks, but the creditors in the East wanted to collect it in specie. In Illinois factional division over the currency policy broke many party ties, and the farmers developed their organization to a strength represented by a large block in national conventions. They declared themselves in favor of retaining greenbacks, and they formed the nucleus of a group of "reckless, broken-down speculators, and equally reckless, broken-down politicians, without any standing in the old parties."[37]

Joseph Kirkland viewed the situation with alarm, but he had little sympathy with speculation of any kind; for as early as 1865 he had announced his distrust of inflated currency and credit. He had recalled his childhood in Michigan with its "distress, the utter absence of specie, the prevalence of the worthless 'Michigan money' (dreadfully scarce, poor as it was); the feeling, deep seated in a small boy's heart, that 'hard times' were the natural state of man and that everything else must be a delusion, foolish, insane, temporary and evanescent." He also had remembered the cartoons he had seen in New York, displaying "a mass of struggling poverty-stricken wretches standing in Wall Street while one building showed the legend, 'Bank. No specie payments made here'; another, 'Custom House. Nothing but specie taken here.' "[38]

Kirkland did not want a recurrence of that situation, and he realized that the two panics were not unlike in many ways. He thought that "to the farmer, who was not in debt, the 'hard times' were less hard than to any other class of persons"; and this was especially true in Illinois where farmers could even get rich in depression times because they could produce immense quantities and buy cheaply.[39] He was concerned with the idea of free silver then beginning to be expressed in the politics of the West, and he noted with care the excitement caused by the demonetization of silver in 1873. Bankers in Chicago raised their voices in vain opposition to the silver movement; the farmers wanted cheap money. Not only the farmers but the banks also had been responsible for inflation, and the farmers wanted at least a distribution of the ill effects.

Kirkland was faced with personal financial difficulties

during the time. He had lost money in the fire of 1871, and he had built an expensive home for his family. Furthermore, he had lost his contract for coal with the Illinois Railway, and he had become involved in a lawsuit with John Shields of Danville concerning some three to five thousand dollars; Kirkland had signed a note for C. E. English, an acquaintance in Tilton, who had bought coal lands. The circumstances surrounding the suit can not now be clearly traced; but Kirkland, ordered to pay the full amount of the note,[40] raised the money and became nearly insolvent. His mines were producing coal, but he could not sell it. He needed some means of earning money until he could again market his coal. Since he was a veteran of the Civil War and since he had some political connections with the Republican Party, he seemingly thought a government job would help him solve his difficulties.

V *Government Employee*

Kirkland went to his old friend, General Webster, head of the internal revenue district in which Chicago was located, and asked for employment. Almost at once he was placed in the central office in Chicago in charge of the division to collect revenue on grains and grain products—and the main product was whiskey;[41] and, in order to prepare himself for the work, he began to study law. His work led him directly into what has since come to be called the "whiskey ring scandal," for it was his office which supplied the government with the information which led to prosecution of offenders.

In Illinois, Cook and Peoria counties supplied sixty per cent of the total amount of distilled spirits produced. The number of distilleries had been reduced somewhat in the period from 1860 to 1870, largely because an excise tax had been placed on distilled spirits in an attempt to increase federal revenue. Because a great amount of grain could not be sold on the market, distilleries to convert it into whiskey were established near the source of supply. At first the imposition of the excise duties had the effect of depressing the business; but gradually, as the probable advance in excise duties became more certain, there was an increase in distilling in order to take advantage of enhanced prices. When the period of speculation was over, there were more distilleries than were needed; and some could no longer continue in business. As early as 1870 or 1871 the distilleries were convinced that they had to enter into an agreement to limit production in order to keep prices up.

Most of the distilleries of Illinois, as well as those of Missouri and Wisconsin, entered into such agreements. The less profitable businesses went out of existence, and the larger ones expanded to replace them by using money which they had saved by making fraudulent returns on their excise taxes. The Treasury Department was aware that distillers had made agreements, but no attempt was made to prosecute them— and no attempt was made to collect taxes which had been evaded. Later, when Benjamin Helm Bristow replaced Richardson in Grant's cabinet as Secretary of the Treasury, he began investigating the tax frauds so openly boasted about in Washington.

The greatest frauds were found to be in St. Louis, Milwaukee, and Chicago; and Bristow started to break up the distillers' system. At the lower levels the frauds involved the gauger, a man placed by the commissioner of internal revenue at the distillery to record the amount of whiskey being made. There were about 2,300 of these men in the internal revenue service, but they were only minor figures involved in the frauds. Above them stood higher officials, reaching as far as party managers, who protected the owners of distilleries from prosecution.

Having money to trace the frauds, Bristow directed the solicitor of the Treasury Department to proceed with an investigation. Distilleries were watched, barrels of whiskey were carefully counted as they left them, the figures were checked against the returns made to the treasury office, and it was quickly discovered that tax-paid spirit stamps were used over and over again. During the years 1874 and 1875, the work of collecting evidence continued; and in May, 1875, a large number of cases was ready for presentation to the Department of Justice. In Chicago, the Internal Revenue Department was in the midst of collecting evidence when Joseph Kirkland entered the office to head a department involved in the work.

The Department of Justice made public the widespread, gigantic tax-evasion frauds; estimates of sums unreported by some firms ran as high as $100,000; and in two years the government had been cheated out of $4,000,000. With the approval of President Grant, prosecutions began at once; and before long, the investigations by the Treasury Department revealed a close connection between the administration and men involved in the frauds. In St. Louis, John McDonald, a close friend of the president, was implicated. In Chicago, evidence indicated that Congressman Charles Farwell and Senator John A. Logan, who had served under Grant in the Union Army and who was now a leader of the Republican Party, were connected with the tax frauds. Obstructions were quickly placed to block prosecutions, and a whispering campaign was begun to make the president mistrust Bristow.

Grant had said: "Let no guilty man escape"; but when evidence indicated that his personal secretary, Babcock, was involved in furthering the interest of the whiskey ring, the president interfered in the prosecution. It was suggested that Babcock, an officer in the army, should be tried by a military tribunal; and Grant, accepting the plan, summoned generals Sheridan, Hancock, and Terry to try the man. On December 9, 1875, the trial began but was soon abandoned; Babcock was brought to trial by the civil court in St. Louis. Grant, having been sworn before the chief justice in Washington, sent testimony to the court which influenced the jury which declared his secretary "not guilty."

The influence of politicians prevented successful prosecution in other cities. In Chicago, Judge Mark Bangs, a former judge of the Illinois Circuit Court, was appointed attorney general in charge of prosecution. He worked hand in hand with the Department of Internal Revenue, and he and Joseph Kirkland became fast friends. When Judge Bangs tried to prosecute the distillers in the Chicago area, he was defeated because testimony which involved Senator Logan was not admitted to court. Others who were involved in the tax frauds were sentenced but soon pardoned. But the public was aroused, for the conspiracy to defraud the government covered the pages of many newspapers. Congress began an examination of the affair.[42]

Joseph Kirkland continued not only his work in the internal revenue offices but his reading of law, which he found most useful. In his free time he also tried to find markets for the coal which his mines were still producing, but he was gradually forced to admit that he was losing money by operating them. In the summer of 1876 when his friend General Webster died, Kirkland was let out of the Internal Revenue Department.[43] Although he tried again to find markets for his coal, he found himself as time passed increasingly in debt. Finally, on February 7, 1877, he filed a voluntary petition of bankruptcy in Circuit Court; and his property, including some lots in Michigan which he had inherited from his father, was assigned to Robert E. Jenkins for sale.[44] At the sheriff's sale which followed, his brother William bought the real estate for twenty-five dollars.[45] The machinery from the coal mines was purchased by the Fountain Coal Mining Company.

Kirkland's dreams of financial independence had vanished. He had lost his job and his business, and he now had to find means to support himself and his family. Since the house in Chicago had remained in his wife's name, he had a roof over his family. His wife would some day inherit money from her father, but he needed immediate assistance. Acting on Judge Bangs' suggestion, he decided to continue the reading of law in the judge's office and to work at the same time as a legal clerk for him. Shortly after Kirkland had started to work for Bangs, the judge was successful in prosecuting the case of J. B. Doyle, who was accused of having forged $200,000 of United States bonds; later, he defended the firm of Roelle, Junker and Company in a case involving excise taxes on whiskey; and in both cases his new clerk helped prepare the evidence.

Because of the recent exposure of the whiskey ring, the firm became the object of public comment; and Joseph Kirkland, in a letter published on January 27, 1877, in the *Chicago Tribune*, not only explained the case but won public support for the firm. Judge Bangs promised to make him a junior partner in the firm as soon as he passed his examination for the bar; but in the meantime, following the custom of the era to allow apprentice lawyers to practice in case work, the judge permitted Kirkland to handle some minor cases. One of these involved testimony before a treasury committee in Washington in connection with a plan to ease the tax on bonds held by insolvent savings banks of Chicago. Kirkland made the most of the opportunity.

The promising industrial revival which had taken place in Chicago after the fire of 1871 had been quickly stopped by the panic of 1873; but, after the first stages of the crisis, a gradual climb back to normal began. But in July, 1877, a series of strikes adversely affected business, and agitation for silver as a legal tender prevented business from expanding. In 1877 eight savings banks of Chicago which had estimated deposits of more than $12,000,000 closed their doors.[46] The causes of the failures were partially rooted in the general panic of 1873, but over-loans and general mismanagement were also responsible. The failures shocked the public, for the savings of hundreds of workers were lost.

Thinking about the financial distress, Joseph Kirkland developed a plan to lift the tax on insolvent saving bonds; and in November, 1877, he presented the plan to the treasury in Washington. When it was adopted, Kirkland became the hero of the hour in Chicago; he was proclaimed a friend of the working classes.[47]

He continued the study of law in the office of Judge Bangs; and in 1880, at the age of fifty, he not only passed the bar examination but led the class examined before the Appellate Court. Judge Bangs at once made him a partner in the law firm.

But Kirkland had long been interested in trying his hand at writing again. In the midst of the depression, even when he was concerned with financial problems, he had tried to write; and he had planned his work in order to take part in activities which were then beginning to form a part of the social and cultural life of the city. His "purpose long dormant" was not haphazardly or instantly achieved, for he had made long preparations to write a novel of western rural life, "following thus at an interval of forty-five years, the path marked out by his mother in her *New Home* in 1840. . . ."[48] But it was still to be five years, however, before "he found that his life work was shaping itself in the way he would have been happy, during all his career to foresee."[49]

Kirkland had begun his practice in writing for *The Prairie Chicken* in 1864; ten years later he had recommenced writing; but it was to be another ten years before his first novel *Zury: The Meanest Man in Spring County* was published. He used the time from 1875 to 1885 to learn as much about writing as possible in the hours he could spare from the business of earning a living.

CHAPTER 3

Miscellaneous Writings

WHEN THE CITY OF CHICAGO began to rebuild after the fire of 1871, the architectural trend followed that of the Second French Empire. With considerable variation of style, the onrush of construction continued over twenty years and resulted eventually in the buildings of the World's Columbian Exposition in 1893. The cultural interests of the people kept pace with this development and with the growth of population, and Joseph Kirkland could indulge in any activity to which his taste inclined. He heard Theodore Thomas and his orchestra in 1869; he attended the Germania Männerchor performance of Karl Maria von Weber's *Der Freischütz;* and he heard the Concordia Music Society perform Mozart's *Magic Flute.* He attended the Gilmore Jubilee, performed in the arches of the new railroad station by the Apollo Club and the Beethoven Club in 1872; and at Crosby's Opera House, the new home of the arts, he heard the Italian Opera Company in *La Traviata, Lucia, Faust,* and *Lohengrin;* and he saw Edwin Booth and Clara Morris in their performances of *Richelieu* and *Camille.* By 1875 the Chicago Academy of Music gave Sunday night concerts and the German choral societies performed regularly; but the old forces of society continued to exist and to challenge the new, more cosmopolitan trends of the city's life.[1]

The years 1874 and 1875 saw a great upheaval of the revival spirit in religion in Chicago, and Moody and Sankey began to hold revival meetings which grew to unprecedented proportions and which brought the old and new forces in the spiritual life of the day into bitter expression in a war between orthodoxy and latitudinarianism. Foremost among the Chicago preachers in the Presbyterian churches was the Reverend David Swing, who was hailed by the liberals in his congregation as a harmonizer of the scientific discoveries of the century with religious faith. But when more conservative and orthodox members of the church disapproved of him, he was accused of heresy.

The Reverend Swing was charged with having delivered lectures to raise funds for a Unitarian chapel and of contributing "to promulgate heresy"; with having used unwarrantable language in regard to Penelope and Socrates; and with having praised the work of John Stuart Mill, "a well-known Atheist." Moreover, Swing did not agree with all the points of Calvinism, so the local synod brought him to trial; and, although he was acquitted, he resigned to begin work for the organization of an "independent central" church.[2] When Joseph Kirkland aided him in his work, the two men became close friends, though Kirkland continued to be a member of Robert Collyer's Unity Church.[3] The two men were also members of the Literary Club, and they worked together until Kirkland's death.[4]

I Experiment in Writing Drama

Literary clubs were not only fashionable in the city but also valuable opportunities for critical discussion among representative groups of men interested in the intellectual growth of Chicago. Kirkland helped organize the Literary Club in 1871, and it was there that he first met James B. Runnion, a Chicago playwright who suggested in 1877 that Kirkland dramatize Alphonse Daudet's *Sidonie*. Kirkland, immediately accepting the idea, thought that the novel might be turned into a drama of morals, but Runnion pointed out that these were of little importance. What was wanted, Runnion said, were action and interest to draw enough people to make the play profitable to the writer and the theater owner. Kirkland, enticed by the prospect of money, began writing the play which he called *The Married Flirt*. When he carried it in finished form to Runnion for criticism and was told that it was too "talkey," Kirkland rewrote it completely; he cut the dialogue, and Runnion thought not only that the play was better but that Kirkland had caught some of the knack of playwrighting.

Kirkland had found the writing very difficult, for it had required that he give infinite pains to details in action and dialogue; but he had learned much from the work. "The two extremes of the literary spectrum," he wrote, "seem to be the essay and the drama. The first is a bronze statue, a mass of homogeneous metal poured hot from the melting pot into a mould previously well prepared to shape it. The drama is a mosaic, a solid through picturesque surface made up of an infinite number of vari-coloured fragments."[6] He had tried in his "mosaic" to keep the tone of Daudet's novel, and the result was that Kirkland complicated his task when he tried to lift dialogue from the novel and at the same time give his actors the semblance of life.

When he had finished the play, a long one of five acts, he carried it to James McVicker, the owner of the McVicker Theatre Company, whose house had been originally opened on November 5, 1857, with a play in which McVicker had played the leading part. Located on Madison Street between State and Dearborn, the theater had burned in 1871; but McVicker had rebuilt it and had reopened it in August, 1872. In 1885 he enlarged it, making it one of the most handsome theater buildings in the United States. But that structure was doomed, for it was destroyed by fire on August 26, 1890. Undaunted, McVicker set about rebuilding, and it again became one of the finest theaters in the country.

To this magnificently stubborn man Kirkland took *The Married Flirt*. When McVicker agreed to produce it, preparations were made at once; and the play opened on December 10, 1877, for a run of two weeks. It was advertised for "every night and a Saturday matinee," with prices of twenty-five cents, fifty cents, seventy-five cents, and one dollar for evening performances, and of twenty-five cents and fifty cents for the matinee.[7] Kirkland had at first thought that he ought to "paper the house"—the custom of giving tickets to friends to assure applause—but he decided not to do so. As he waited anxiously for the first performance, he noted that a novel writer could say farewell to his characters at the end of his work; a writer of drama had to watch his characters come to life.

Geraldine Mays, a popular actress cast in the leading role, was supported by Roland Reed, Harry Pearson, and J. H. Mc-Vicker.[8] The play contained "some very pretty and attractive scenic effects, and the audience was well pleased." Miss Mays was admired as the daughter of a "Tragedian," which she played in a "sweet, natural and very effective style." But to Kirkland's great surprise the play, which he had thought would teach a moral lesson, was received by some of the religious people of the city with apprehension. A storm of criticism broke in the *Tribune,* and in it "Legitimist" in an open letter to McVicker declared that there were "sound arguments" against producing a piece which portrayed a marked woman as a flirt who escaped punishment for her immoral actions; such plays, he asserted, taught bad habits to weak persons.[9]

McVicker, no man to receive such criticism in silence, denounced the letter in a strong reply:

> I am fond of a good laugh, and a moderate joke will cause me to smile loudly. Your correspondent "Legitimist" is a huge joke, though I doubt if he has sense enough to know it. He evidently intended his learned epistle for me, and there is just enough femininity in my nature to "talk back" when occasion calls. How relieved the dramatic critic of *The Tribune* must have felt to have "Legitimist" come to his aid and help stamp "The Married Flirt, Sidonie," as an "exhibition of moral depravity," with such sound arguments. The "sound arguments," as may be said, begin with a statement that "Legitimist" has not himself seen "Sidonie"—which admission does somewhat weaken his case as a critic.
>
> I really must produce something to please this moral element of our city, of which "Legitimist" is spokesman. Perhaps the fairy extravaganza in preparation for the holidays will suit, as it is "childlike and bland," and I may, by placing pull back dresses on my little fairies (they are children) prevent his being shocked by viewing their le—understandings. This is long enough.[10]

Kirkland kept silent. His play had offended one of the elements of the city which he respected, for he was always concerned with moral effects; but he also remembered Runnion's statement that morals didn't matter but that the money which a play made did. Kirkland made little from his play; for when it folded, he lamented the fact that he had received only twenty-five cents an hour for his work.[11] It was his last attempt at playwrighting; for, as a result of his failure, he determined to spend his time trying to produce fiction or essays.

II *Literary Clubs*

Kirkland's literary endeavors were stimulated by the Twentieth Century Club, which he also helped to found. Sponsored by Mrs. George H. Grant, who had lived on the Atlantic coast for some time and who had been a member of the Nineteenth Century Club of New York, the club was founded to give its members the opportunity to enjoy contact with men and women in the world of art, science, literature, and statesmanship. Mrs. Grant, inspired by the ideas such a club could afford, had gathered together prospective members on November 16, 1889. Included in the group were not only Joseph Kirkland but also William Morton Payne, the editor of *Dial*, one of Chicago's literary magazines. These two men were asked to draft the by-laws of the organization, which held a total of fifty-one meetings from the time of its founding until its disbanding in 1916.[12] The first speaker engaged by the club was Charles Dudley Warner, a friend of Kirkland's from the days when Caroline Kirkland's house in New York had been the gathering place of literary people. John Masefield was the last speaker; others were Thomas Hughes, Matthew Arnold, Sir Henry Irving, and Henry James.

Kirkland also belonged to the Saracen Club, which had been organized in 1876 for the purpose of criticizing ideas and literature as unsparingly as "the Saracens fought their enemies and giving as little quarter."[13] There Kirkland came to know Henry B. Fuller and Samuel Willard, who sponsored the club, and other writers of Chicago. At one meeting Kirkland read a paper on realism; and Mary Hartwell Catherwood, a club member and a novelist from one of the suburbs, interrupted his reading to disagree with him about the duties of a novel writer. Catherwood's books, which concerned the French occupation of the Mississippi Valley, proved her to be an out-and-out romanticist—and so did her objections to Kirkland's paper. Kirkland declared that a novelist could deal only with life as he knew it if he fulfilled his obligations to his readers; and, in the hot discussion which followed, so much time slipped by that he was not able to finish his paper. The paper may have contained a full explanation of Kirkland's theory of fiction, but unfortunately it has disappeared.

Kirkland also belonged to the Papyrus Club, which he joined in September, 1891. Writers only were eligible for membership, and among its members were Maud Menefre, a writer of children's stories; Thomas S. Denison, the playwright; Nancy Huston Banks, who was known for her stories of Kentucky romance; and Moses P. Handy.

In 1893 Kirkland, already known as a writer of some standing, became a member of the Contributor's Club. Organized under the sponsorship of Mr. and Mrs. Charles Herotin, the club was to "hold but two or three meetings a season" to allow members to read examples of their literary work. The first meeting took place in February, 1893, at the Herotin's house at 65 Bellevue Place. About seventy people joined the club, and among them were Hobart C. Chatfield-Taylor; Harriet C. Moss; Lucy Monroe and her younger sister Harriet; Arthur J. Eddy, who agreed to edit a magazine in which the literary efforts of the club members who appeared on the programs would be preserved; and Caroline Kirkland, Joseph's eldest daughter. The Potter Palmers became members, and the William Armours joined, for Mrs. Armour had become interested in the literary activities of the city. Henry Blake Fuller, who had not yet produced any of his important novels, though he published *The Cliff-Dwellers* that year (1893), joined the club; and so did David Swing, the ex-Presbyterian minister whose "Central Church" had become the gathering place of the fashionable society of Chicago.[14]

Figaro, one of the little magazines of Chicago at that time, reported the February gathering; and it noted that the club spent enough money on its magazine to "endow an asylum for Geniuses who failed because they did not have 'Pull'." *Figaro* also reported that Joseph Kirkland had read a sketch at the first meeting and that afterwards, when he was told by one of the women members that his sketch had always been one of her favorite pieces, he remarked: "Ah, yes, she's a charming woman, but—I'm afraid she doesn't read our books." Acquaintance with literature, the magazine's reporter remarked, was no prerequisite for membership in the club.

III *Reviews, Articles, and Poetry*

Kirkland evidently spent much time at his clubs, and it is probable that he talked to most of the budding writers of the city. His association with William Morton Payne brought him an invitation to contribute some book reviews to *Dial*. Accepting, Kirkland began his miscellaneous publication in that and other magazines with a review of *The Diary and Letters of Frances Burney* for the June, 1880, issue of *Dial*.[16] Noting the lively style of Miss Burney, the friend of Samuel Johnson, Kirkland pointed to the fact that her detailed pictures, little facts, and pert observations reproduce for readers the life of eighteenth-century London. He thought that novelists might learn something worth while from the realistic reporting of the diary and the letters of the Blue Stocking—the daughter of a well-known London physician and, later, when she married a Frenchman and became Madame D'Arblay, a well-traveled woman.

In August, 1880, Kirkland reviewed Benjamin Abbott's *Judge and Jury* for the *Dial*;[17] and, after noting the strange customs of lawyers and courts and the humor and the curiosities found in legal practices, he suggested that they were remains from more ancient customs. For the October, 1880, *Dial*, he wrote of Albion Tourgée's *Bricks Without Straw*, which he rightly deemed a partisan romance built without enough plot to hold it together.[18] In summarizing the story, he showed that Tourgée had manipulated his material in order to have all things prove the South to be immoral and depraved. He asserted that Tourgée was not a good novelist: he was not objective enough, his work was too preachy, and he destroyed effect by long personal harangues about the evil consequences of slavery upon the people of the South. He also noted, as modern critics have done, that Tourgée's self-righteousness affected his writing; he had turned out a piece which reflected the narrowness of attitude of the Northern religious reformer who had attempted to transplant his practices in the South after the Civil War.

Kirkland continued to write book reviews for the *Dial*, and the larger parts of them dealt with plot or with the ideas found in the books he reviewed. In March, 1881, he published a review of George F. Seward's *Chinese Immigration*,[19] a work which emphasized the dangers of unlimited Oriental immigration; and he followed that review with one of George B. McClellan's *The Peninsular Campaign of General McClellan*,[20] in which he adopted the author's view that the campaign failed largely because of Lincoln's withdrawal of McDowell's troops from the campaign. In July, 1881, when he wrote about *The Correspondence of Prince Talleyrand and King Louis XVIII During the Congress of Vienna*,[21] he discussed the corrupt state into which early nineteenth-century diplomacy had fallen.

In December, 1883, Kirkland turned to *The Autobiography of Anthony Trollope*.[22] He admired Trollope's style, but he thought the English novelist might profit from writing works less romantic in tone. Trollope was, Kirkland mistakenly concluded, merely another English romantic of a type already too numerous. He may have been influenced in his assessment of Trollope by the furor which William Dean Howells and realism were creating at the time in both Europe and America. At any rate, Kirkland did no more reviewing for three years; but in August, 1886, he returned to *Dial* with a review of the third part of Tolstoy's *War and Peace*;[23] in it Kirkland joined Howells in the war against romanticism.

Howells had begun his "Editor's Study" in *Harper's* in January, 1886, and Kirkland had no doubt followed the articles with avid interest, for he was forming something of an opinion of realism for himself. In his review of Tolstoy's work, Kirkland asserted that the writer gave perfect pictures of Russian life. "The only open question on them is, are the subjects worth the canvas?" he wrote. The pictures, examples of the photographic school of realism, would grow in worth, he declared, for they gave an idea of life in an era when nobles owned the serf's body and soul. The work was "realistic—photographic—almost microscopic," but "on the whole it reminds the reader of the Pre-Raphaelite who wanted to paint the Rocky Mountains life-size. . . . The difficulty in [the] realistic novel . . . is in knowing what to omit. Much detail is good. Too much detail is intolerable." Feeling that Tolstoy sometimes lost his sense of perspective and that in "such places the author's fancy runs away with him," Kirkland cited the chapters from *War and Peace* about Freemasonry as examples.

Nevertheless, he felt that "these Russian novels mark an era in literature. The romantic and realistic are engaged in a life-and-death struggle. It is their Waterloo and lo, on the eastern horizon appears a Blücher, with a force which must decide the battle in favor of realism . . . ," for the time had come to set up new canons of art. "Photographic exactitude in scene-painting—phonographic literalness in dialogue—telegraphic realism in narration—these are the new canons for the art of fiction," Kirkland declared as he began to set forth some of his own concepts of writing. "Whether this is a novelty or only a restoration, it were bootless to inquire. Kismet—it is fate. Perhaps the highest of art is shown by a return to nature. Certainly some of Tolstoi's 'local color' (as he portrays the patriarch and bondsmen of wild Russia) is *naif* enough to remind the reader of the simplicity of the oldest of narratives: 'And Abraham sat in his tent-door in the heat of the day.'" Furthermore, he added, "Such books as Tolstoi's make the careful observer suspect that unless English fiction can shake off some of the iron trammels that bind it, it must yield all hope of maintaining its long-held supremacy."

In this review Kirkland had reached for a theory of literature; but in his next review for the *Dial,* in April, 1887, he returned to history with F. A. Walker's *History of the Second Army Corps in the Army of the Potomac,*[24] which he praised for successful recording of facts for the consumption of persons at a later date. Kirkland also used the review to voice once more his defense of McClellan's role in the Peninsular Campaign and to blame Lincoln for its failure because he kept McDowell's army in Washington. In the *Dial* for October, 1887, he considered Moses C. Tyler's *Patrick Henry*[25] to be a fine reconstruction of fundamental, factual history; he noted Professor Tyler's wide acquaintance with the period in which the work was laid and praised the book as a picture of life as it was in the days of the colonial struggle for independence.

Kirkland's last three reviews for the *Dial* also dealt with works of history. In April, 1888, he wrote about Charles B. Mackham's *Lives of Sir Francis and Sir Horace Vere;*[26] in October, 1889, he reviewed I. A. F. de Bourrienne's *Memories of Napoleon Bonaparte*, which portrayed Napoleon as a conceited tyrant;[27] and in May, 1893, he ended his reviews with one of John C. Rope's *The Campaign of Waterloo*, which Kirkland regarded as a full and excellent treatment of a major military battle.[28]

While Kirkland was writing these book reviews, he also was writing poetry and some short stories. In March, 1892, two short stories, "Tell the Sentry to Load with Ball Cartridges," a story of the Civil War, and "Meet and Fitting," a sketch of gullible citizens of Chicago, appeared in *Figaro*.[29] "Peg-Leg Sullivan," a sketch of a dock hand who had lost a leg in the Civil War, was also accepted by *Figaro* in April, 1892.[30] In September, 1893, *McClure's Magazine* printed "The Surgeon's Miracle,"[31] a short story in dialect, the first of Kirkland's sustained attempts to show character by using this device.

One other sketch appeared after Kirkland's death. "Was Its Best Fencer," which was published in the *Chicago Tribune* on May 27, 1894, dealt with an officer who forced his men to chop firewood rather than tear down a rail fence. One unpublished story, "One Clergyman and One Suburban Maid," described a minister who, having denounced a wealthy member of his congregation for her treatment of servants, was forced by her to resign his pulpit.[32] Kirkland, concerned with the rights of all individuals, may have written the story as the result of an actual incident which had come to his attention, for he also wrote articles about human rights.

Among these articles expressing his humanitarian ideas is one Kirkland published in *Scribner's Magazine;*[33] a descriptive sketch, "Among the Poor in Chicago" is about the slum area. Kirkland recorded the inadequacy of housing, the lack of food, and the immorality which he associated with debility caused by the consumption of liquor; but he had little to suggest to alleviate the conditions. In another article about the same subject in the *Critic* of November, 1893, noting that "at the fair one met at every turn some form of bodily disability or deformity," he was impressed with the kindness of

Helen Keller's "wingless guardian angel."[34] Other subjects also interested him, and in August, 1892, he turned to history for an article about the Chicago fire of 1871 which he published in *The New England Magazine*.[35] Recalling the havoc and destruction of the fire, he pointed with pride to the rebuilding of the city as one of the great accomplishments in the annals of history.

Trying his hand at all types of literary activity, he even wrote some poetry. In 1883 Kirkland published the poem, "The Lady or the Tiger? or Both?" in *Century Magazine*.[36] Written as a humorous comment about Frank R. Stockton's short story, "The Lady or the Tiger?", the poem retells the story of a young man who dared tell the daughter of an Eastern king of his love for her and whose audacity brought swift retaliation from the king. Placed in an arena, the young man had the choice of opening one of two doors—one hiding a beautiful dancer and the other a man-eating tiger. Stockton left the reader to decide for himself which door the young man opened; Kirkland revised the story by having the tiger tear through the wall separating him from the young lady and eat her. As a result, the young man faced a tiger no matter which door he opened. But the tiger, now surfeited, wanted no more food; and he passed the young man by, thus permitting a happy ending for the lover, who was saved for his sweetheart, the king's daughter. The poem is not great, but it is clever. Using every possible device to make the line endings rhyme, he produced a piece of wit of a kind familiar to the readers of that day.

Another poem about stupidity appeared in the *Contributor's Magazine* for May, 1894.[37] Composed in 1876, it was used in a memorial to Kirkland after his death. One other poem came from his pen in these years. Addressed to his wife, it was dated May 17, 1893, and was called "Glorious Eyes."[38] Written in closed couplets, it details the moods which the lady's eyes create in her admirer. A love poem which expressed too much of his personal sentiment for his wife, Kirkland did not publish it.

In addition to these works, Kirkland published some chapters of his novels as short stories. In *America* for May, 1888, he selected "The Captain of Company K," which is contained in the first chapter of his novel of the same name.[39] In December of the same year he published "Christmas of a Quarter-Century Ago," which is found in chapters fifteen and sixteen of his novel *The Captain of Company K;*[40] and in the same issue chapters seven and eight of the novel were published as "Under Fire."[41] Much of the material which he used in "Christmas a Quarter-Century Ago" was drawn from his own memory, which was supplemented by a sketch of his mother's, "Old Thoughts on the New Years," which had appeared in her work *Western Clearings.*[42] One other chapter from a novel, "Zury's $1000 Blunder" from *The McVeys* appeared in *Ehrich's Quarterly* for October, 1887.[43]

About 1890, Kirkland became the literary editor for the *Chicago Tribune;* his task was to select the stories to be used in the Sunday supplement. He published no signed work in the paper except a series of letters which were written from Central America during a trip with the Warner Miller expedition to examine Lake Nicaragua as a site for a canal across the isthmus. Kirkland, invited to go with the group as a special correspondent for the *Tribune,* reported the progress of the party which Warner G. Miller, head of the party and the president of the Nicaragua Canal Company, had organized in 1891 with a view toward promotion of sales of stock. Sailing from New York on March 14, 1891, the party was delayed by bad weather and reached Greytown on April 3. There the steamer was wrecked; and, after having been rescued, the party continued to cross the isthmus to the Pacific. Kirkland's letters detail the customs and habits of the natives, the beauty of the countryside, and the lack of progress among native workingmen. After the expedition had reached the Pacific, Kirkland returned to Chicago in May, 1891.[44]

Kirkland's miscellaneous work gave him some opportunity to express his ideas about all sorts of subjects; but it also served in no small degree to help him arrive at a theory of literature which he would not fully express until after his most important work in the field of fiction had been completed. And, when he began to write his novels, he tried to practice something of the theory which he believed he had derived from his mother's work. As a result, he became a part of the movement of realism in literature which produced the principal writers of the last quarter of the nineteenth century.

CHAPTER 4

Literary Theory

WHEN JOSEPH KIRKLAND, age fifty, had passed the bar examination and could face a life relatively free from financial worries, he turned to the writing of fiction which carried out the aims which his mother had expressed in her sketches of the 1830's and 1840's. He had lived through the half-century which was marked by the most important productions in romantic writing in the United States; he had participated in the Civil War which had disjointed the country; and he had experienced something of the disillusionment of the promise of the West. He brought from his experiences and observations a first-hand knowledge of the times, and he had an intense desire to re-examine the meaning of life in America. He realized that the Civil War had brought changes in emphasis about life and its processes and its meanings as expressed in literature, and he felt that he might be able to record what he knew if he could write a novel which would be a study of society as he had seen it—although he intended to conceal the study with as much artistry as possible. He turned, naturally, to fictional realism as the means by which he could most aptly succeed in carrying out his talent. And he showed himself to be a part of his times in so doing.

I *Background: Aspects of Realism*

In a general way, one may say that from 1830—the year of Joseph Kirkland's birth—to 1860, the dominant trend in literature in America was romantic. But the vast changes— social and economic, religious and aesthetic, literary and philosophical—which were brought about by the Civil War and by the advance of science put an end to romanticism as the main trend: and little by little the emphasis changed from romanticism to realism and naturalism. The change, it is true, came about largely through the espousal of realism by William Dean Howells, Mark Twain, and Henry James; but it had been introduced by the local colorists, and some of them later looked to these greater writers for encouragement in their attempt to create a truly native literature.[1]

The life of the pioneer, with its lack of reverence for tradition which was not its own creation; the barren social life of the frontier; the use of humor as a weapon of social criticism—all these contributed to the demand to present life truthfully. Too, the movement in science created a similar movement in literature—a scientific attitude in writing; and the European realists—Zola, Turgenev, and Tolstoy—gave impetus to the "truthful presentation of material" in fiction. Such presentation encouraged the recognition of unconventional interpretations of life, the use of transcriptions of dialect, and the stripping away of glamor and romance to reveal the crass materialism which was the Gilded Age.

Writers of realistic fiction sought to subordinate all the influences which they felt to the whole of their work—to place facts of the immediate present before the reader. Though most of the workers in realism had faith in human nature and were, in the main, optimistic, they sought to see life in terms of what it might have been as well as in terms of what it was; and they fell sometimes into sentimentalism in their efforts to make the contrast. But they sought to bring about reform by revealing the unvarnished present, and they wrote with the highest sincerity to hasten the coming of the future golden day. They aimed also at national characters in order to produce a national literature, and they reproduced the quality of texture and background which they knew first-hand from experience and observation. They tried to be entirely indigenous, unromantic, and true to emotion—vivid and strong. Their original contacts with men and nature, rough-hewn as the logs which went into the pioneer cabins, built the vital sense of life itself; and, as the logs of a cabin determined its shape, so too did the material of life determine the character of the fiction which they wrote.

The aim of the writers was to find free and easy design wherein event could follow event without the hampering effect of intrigue. Form had to be organic—novels were to grow naturally, allowing the characters and their situations to dictate the growth, so that the world could be pictured, not as low and revolting, but as possibly agreeable, attractive, and lofty. Therefore, the writers felt that nothing vague and undefined could contribute to artistic writing. The occasional places, the habitual moods, the tiresomeness of everyday life must be used as the basis of writing. Accuracy in recording the living speech of men and women, the settings and images, and the characters (the central emphasis always) formed the intent of the writer of realism; and he could, therefore, be individual in drawing his power, his forms, and his views from the society in which he lived and observed and which he also recorded. For the writers meant to look straight at life as it is without enameling it with gaudy colors. They meant to teach, as Zola had said, but only by painting life truly; and Howells echoed and reechoed the aims. For to most of the writers of realism, writing was only the remembering of the history of their own lives or observations; and they tended toward perceptions of cultural relativity, objectivity, and the penetration of the textures and patterns which they knew. In their intent to be faithful to their materials, they tried to project the mind and morality of the American with whom they lived.

Most realists looked to Howells as mentor, for he had formulated a theory which included the use of the commonplace, the idea that character is more important than plot, an attitude toward morals, the idea that realism was the expression of democracy, and the attack on romanticism. As a result the realists used the theory of social stages to portray character—the idea, as Frederick Jackson Turner later expressed it, that society developed on the frontier in terms of process, development, and evolution as the result of the influence of environment in selecting and adapting forms. They tried to tie character revelation together by episodes carefully selected, if they were disciplined writers; or they piled them high in manuscript if they were not. And they often wrote in their spare moments, when, like Edgar Watson Howe, they could put aside the labor of earning a living to concentrate their efforts on producing stark realism which was often made more stark by the very weariness of the writers themselves. Yet they strove to reveal the truth in terms of environmental influences upon the process of interaction among the people, places, and cultures of which they wrote.

The vogue of Taine's deterministic formula—according to which literature or art, like natural phenomena, is the by-product of *time, place,* and *race*—had already been put into practice, however imperfectly, by Edward Eggleston in his fictional reports of life in Indiana and by the beginning of the practice of criticism to describe rather than to appraise. Too, the influence of Howells and of his definition of realism as "fidelity to experience and probability of nature," "the quest for the not very high or the not very low," and the use of the habitual and the average had impressed the writers of the period who wanted to transcribe life as faithfully as they could. Furthermore, the aftermath of the Civil War, with its memories of death and destruction, was revealed with fidelity to fact in the work of writers such as John De Forest; and the readjustments and poverty and unrest which came after the war were already a part of the materials of fiction.

The theories of science certainly affected the work of the realists. The stress of chance which had been a part of the creed of the "hard" evolutionists; the ruthless competition and the survival of the fittest which had been stated and pointed up by Spencer and Sumner; the Unitarian stress on "second causes"; and the new studies in geology, biology, and the psychic factors in the life of man—all of these brought to the writers of the age an impetus to apply similar techniques to their fiction. The ideas of social reform from the outside to the inside, of Christian charity, of the extension of the arguments against chattel slavery, and of the concept of the individual isolated in an alien universe affected in varying degree the thought and work of all the writers of realism. Among those writers who were thus affected and who tried to express their own theories of fiction was Joseph Kirkland whose explanation was made after he had already completed his work in fiction and knew, therefore, from actual experience some of the difficulties which the writer of realism encountered.

II *Kirkland's Theory of Literary Realism*

The major works of Joseph Kirkland were attempts to put into practice a literary theory which he had developed over a long period of time. He had been interested in realism since his mother had written her sketches of Michigan life; he had used that theory to criticize Tolstoy's work by pointing to the need for simplicity in the selection of detail by the realistic novelist; and in the *Dial* in 1893 he made the most complete explanation of his ideas on writing fiction.[2] "*Let only truth be told, and not all the truth*," he began, and he italicized to stress his words. Continuing, he wrote: "These ten words seem to me to be the true creed-and-ten-commandments for modern prose writers."

Earlier works, he thought, were too fanciful—too full of heroes and godlike creatures; they were the result of the adolescence of the human race. The last half of the nineteenth century had brought changes; the iconoclasts Tolstoy, Daudet, Ibsen, and Hardy had destroyed romance and had substituted real flesh and blood for romantic persons.

Kirkland felt that much truth was not worth telling; that some truth could not properly be told; but that each author had to decide where to draw the line. He noted that Tolstoy sometimes went beyond the line—especially for English-speaking peoples who stood first "in morality, delicacy, and decency, in its prose fiction." Hardy, Howells, and their ilk wrote only books which all members of a family might properly read; and Kirkland approved entirely of the line concerning the truth proper to be told which each of those writers drew for himself. But of all authors, Daudet and de Maupassant, the French writers, showed "the most perfect perception of the line of limitation in prose fiction." However, their countrymen, Flaubert and Zola, went beyond the line of propriety into indecency; for they were not discriminating enough in their selection of truth to leave out the trivial or the improper. Yet, he felt, the writer must have photographic exactitude in scene painting, phonographic literalness in dialogue, telegraphic realism in narration. Knowing what to omit was the greatest difficulty facing the writer. But, in spite of the faults which he found in most writers, Kirkland felt that all the writers of realism had discarded romantic fancy and had contributed to the moral progress of mankind.

Such moral uplifting of mankind "from lower to higher" as the world came to realism step by step indicated to Kirkland that intellectual progress had kept pace with material progress. Realism placed man on top of the pinnacle which he had built. It was not "naked and crude," for "the strong truth itself is not digestible until it has passed through the alembic of genius"—a thought Kirkland emphasized in the closing paragraph of his article on literary theory. "Let only truth be told, and not all the truth," he wrote again. "Millions of truths are barred, and all vague, vast depths of untruth are barred." He then added: "These barriers established, there remains between them a starry firmament of illimitable light which the mind of man has discerned and the spectroscope and camera of prose have made available for each of us."

Kirkland tied his theory to the work with which he was familiar, the major writers of realism of his day; and he tried to carry his theory into practice in his novels. What truths might not be used were not made specific, for Kirkland relied on the taste of the writer to establish proper limits. Yet there can be no question but that he believed that there were some truths which were not possible materials for revealing life fiction in his day because of the prudery of the reading audience. He would do away with conventions which smacked of falsehood, for such conventions were, in his opinion, indecent. And, there can be no doubt that he referred to his own theory of realism as the direct outgrowth and continuation of his mother's literary theory when he wrote that after "an interval of forty-five years" he had followed "the path marked out by his mother in her *New Home.* . . ."

CHAPTER 5

Zury: The Meanest Man in Spring County

E ARLY IN THE SPRING of 1883 Joseph Kirkland sent his his wife and four children to Europe where they remained until the fall of 1884. After renting the house on Rush Street in Chicago to the Blair family, he moved his belongings to the attic of his sisters' house at 275 Huron Street; there he began to write his first novel.[1] He hoped, as he later wrote in his autobiographical sketch, to carry out "a purpose long dormant in his mind, by writing a novel of Western rural life. . . . Following . . . the path marked out by his mother." Selecting the farm life of Illinois in the pre-Civil War years as his subject, he built his work from his own experiences, acquaintances, events, and localities; for he intended to tell "the truth unadorned and unvarnished."[2]

By December, 1886, Kirkland had finished his work on the novel; had sent it to Houghton, Mifflin and Company, of Boston, who had returned it for revisions; and was ready to send it revised back to the company for publication. Kirkland had originally drawn from his mother's sketches to make his work a more authentic picture of early frontier life, and he had piled sheet upon sheet of manuscript until he had written of the early life of Zury Prouder, of Anne McVey, of Anne's twins—one of whom, Phil (the boy, inclined to mechanical genius), became the first engineer on the *Pioneer,* the first steam engine of the Galena and Chicago Railroad. He had ended the novel abruptly with an account of Phil's death in a collision on the road.[3] In his revision Kirkland reduced the amount of material which he had previously included.

He deleted chapters dealing with the Galena and Chicago Railroad, and he wrote a transition to the last chapter of the novel in which he brought Zury and Anne together in marriage. He noted that the story of Phil and his engine was another story not yet written in full, and he began to rewrite it as *The McVeys*. Hence, *The McVeys: An Episode* is reworked material which Kirkland removed in his revision of *Zury* before the novel was published.

I *The Story*

The story of Zury Prouder opens when his father, Ephraim Prouder, a veteran of the War of 1812, brings his family to Wayback, Illinois, to take up government land. The family—Ephraim, his wife Selina, and their two children, Usury, called "Zury," and a daughter known simply as "li'l Shoog"—has traveled from the mountains of southern Pennsylvania to find a new home in the West. The Prouders seek a new life which they believe will bring the success which they did not find in their old home. They locate the site of their new home; and, before winter, they build a log cabin. Much of the work is done by the boy Zury, for the father has no imagination and no inventiveness. The winter brings want and hardship, and in the midst of it, the little girl, unable to survive the rigors of the new life, dies.

The death of the girl changes the other members of the family. The mother does not long survive, and Ephraim becomes increasingly dependent on Zury. Zury himself has been hardened by the death of his little sister, for he had decided that the girl would not have died had the family had money. Money, therefore, becomes the most important thing in his life, and he hardens his natural instincts, forcing them into a determination to get money at any costs. His natural ability and imagination aid him, and he soon becomes known in the community for his hard work and his shrewdness in business affairs. He turns every opportunty into a business gain; and, when he decides to marry, he selects a neighbor girl, Mary Peddicomb. She will bring him land; she is a hard worker; she will be easily managed. Zury soon becomes the richest man in the community.

As the richest man in the neighborhood, Zury is elected to many public offices. Such offices pay no salary, but Zury manages them in the same efficient manner in which he handles his own affairs. Especially does he pay attention to his duties as a member of the school board, for he feels his lack of education keenly; and, though he dominates the other members of the board, he wishes to find the best possible teacher for the children of the community. He encourages John McVey—who had tried to teach the school but had been forced out of the job by older students whom he could not control—to send to Boston for Anne Sparrow, a young lady who wants to find a new life in Illinois. McVey, who has become a clerk in the local inn, sends for the girl; when she arrives, he becomes her close friend and adviser. But his place as adviser is soon taken by Zury Prouder.

Anne is hired by the school board only after Zury has thrown the weight of his influence behind her, but he forces her to accept a reduced salary. However, when she decides that she does not want to "board round" the neighborhood, Zury suggests that she use one of the rooms of the school-house as her home; and Anne, following his suggestion that she persuade Eureka Anstey, one of her older pupils, to live with her, moves into the schoolhouse. Anne is grateful to Eureka for her help and presence, for Anne is the victim of a psychological fear of the dark.

The fear of the dark which possesses Anne becomes the turning point in the story when Zury, whose first wife has died, asks Anne and her friend John McVey to a community picnic across the river. After a successful outing the three start home, but on the way they run into a prairie fire. McVey is sent back with the horses and carriage, and Anne and Zury start for home on foot. They find they must detour because of the fire, and by the time they reach the river Anne is exhausted. Her old fear of the dark returns. When Zury starts to swim the river, thus leaving her alone, she develops all the cunning of a psychotic to keep him with her. He mistakes her action for passion and spends the night with her. The next morning they make their separate ways home.

Zury, worried that Anne may try to get him to marry her, hastily marries the sister of his dead wife; he not only protects himself but acquires more land at the same time. Anne, discovering that she is pregnant, is forced to appeal to him for help when a mob burns an old stump in which she has hidden her money. Zury, impressed by the fact that she does not blame him any more than she blames herself for the situation, suggests that she marry John McVey, which she does after she has told him the truth. John, who secures a job through Zury's influence, takes Anne to Springville to live; but he does not remain long in the story; he is a ne'er-do-well who before long seeks his fortune in California where he conveniently dies of fever and leaves Anne a widow with a set of twins, Phil and Meg. Only Anne and Zury are now aware of the real father of the children.

The children attract Zury; his children by his legal wives have died almost as soon as they were born. He craftily manages to have his wife suggest to Anne that they are willing to adopt the boy, but Anne will not accept the offer. But the offer does establish friendly relations between Anne and Mrs. Prouder with the result that Anne is asked to spend some time visiting the Prouders in order to help Zury plan speeches during an election campaign in which he is a candidate for the legislature. With Anne's help Zury wins the election.

Zury, expecting the legislature to be as efficient as he is in his personal affairs, is soon disillusioned by politics. He works hard to stem the tide of reckless waste without success, but his work wins him a reputation for honesty and efficiency. He spends much time away from home trying to do his job as legislator; and, during his term, his wife Flora, who had never received much attention from him, sickens and dies. Zury, tired of politics, does not seek re-election but turns instead to business and farming; and he turns as well to Anne Sparrow McVey whom he has decided to marry.

Because she has little use for Zury, Anne rejects his proposal. Zury feels the refusal deeply; but, realizing that his grasping nature has been responsible for Anne's decision, he decides to change. After a period of time, when he has changed a good deal, Anne softens in her attitude and accepts him.

The last chapter of the novel presents a picture of Anne and Zury after they have married and after a considerable period of time has passed. The twins are grown and have gone into their own work, and their place is taken by another child, Willie. Zury and Anne have traveled, and Zury has become almost a country squire in dress and interests. He is a source of help and advice to his neighbors, and his faith in humanity is restored. He has regained the natural impulses toward kindliness which he had as a boy. He has risen through the social stages of the frontier from poverty to gentility.

The story is told on two levels: it is the story of the rise of Zury Prouder, and it is the story of the melodramatic romance of Anne and Zury. The latter is imposed on the former in order to provide a love interest. Yet the two levels are closely connected, for the love story aids the character development, even though the romantic plot is at times so unbelievable that were it not for Kirkland's faithfulness to setting and dialogue one could hardly accept it at all. Kirkland hoped that the two levels of the story which he created would help make the novel popular with the reading audiences of the day.

II Publication and Hamlin Garland

Kirkland waited eagerly for *Zury* to be accepted, published, and reviewed; and on January 20, 1887, he wrote to his family in Europe that it had not yet appeared. In March, 1887, *Zury* was accepted for publication, and in May it was released. One of the first reviews was written by Hamlin Garland, who wrote: "The full realization of the inexhaustible wealth of native American material . . . will come to the Eastern reader with the reading of *Zury*. It is as native to Illinois as Tolstoy's *Anna Karenina* and Torguenieft's *Father and Sons* are to Russia, its description are so infused with life and so graphic. The book is absolutely unconventional—not a trace of old-world literature or society—and every character is new and native. . . . The central figure is Zury. This is a great and consistent piece of character painting."[4]

The review so pleased Joseph Kirkland that he wrote Garland to thank him, and Garland wrote back to say that he was a Western man and that he intended shortly to make a trip west to see his parents. Kirkland invited him to stop in Chicago, and Garland accepted the invitation.[5] On May 31, 1887,

Kirkland wrote Garland that he had received his second letter. He added that some people had hinted that the author of *Zury* was a woman because the character of Anne had suggested to them that only a female could have written the book. "I was not pained by the suggestion that the author . . . was a woman," Kirkland wrote. "Rather the contrary. What hurt me was the suggestion that the book is coarse in its tendency." He complained that one notice had criticized adversely the rough character, the dialect, and the suggestiveness which he had used to build the sexual relations of Anne and Zury.

In his next letter of June 7, 1887, Kirkland told Garland that he had used Howe's *Annals* [sic] *of a Country Town* as an example—and a warning. He thought that work too melancholy and too dark, and he had tried to avoid such absolute gloom of tone and atmosphere. He must have been aware, however, that the early years of Zury were painted in dark colors; for, as Howells pointed out later, the death of "little Shoog" is indeed a black picture. Kirkland also told Garland that he was still at work on a story of Phil; if he could finish it and write another about the Civil War, he would be ready to quit writing fiction.

On June 7, Kirkland wrote to Garland to urge him to come to Chicago before June 17 because Mrs. Kirkland and the children would leave the city on that date to spend the summer in Michigan. Kirkland also suggested that some readers believed his book to be immoral because they thought Anne Sparrow had the suggestion of a wanton about her. In answer Garland evidently inquired what Kirkland intended to write next, for Kirkland replied that he did not expect to do a novel of modern times; he hoped to take the boy, Phil, through the war, "using my memory to bring up some startling and heart-rending realistic scenes." But before he could do that work, Kirkland noted, he must put Phil "through his fortunes on his engines."

Garland did not arrive as soon as Kirkland hoped, and Kirkland wrote to his wife in Michigan on June 22 to say that his friend had been delayed.[6] To his daughter Ethel he wrote on June 29 that Garland had not yet arrived;[7] and he also wrote to his sister-in-law, Dorothy Wilkinson, in Syracuse, on the same day to say that Garland had not yet come.[8] Garland did arrive in Chicago on the evening of July 2, and he went straight to Kirkland's house on Rush Street. He had been riding for two nights and a day in a day coach; when he knocked at the Kirkland door, he was tired and had a bad headache.

In his later works Garland recorded not only his first reactions to *Zury* but also his impressions of Kirkland:

> When in 1886 Hurd asked me to review a novel called "Zury" . . . and I found it recording the dialect of the early Illinois "sucker" I tackled it with some misgivings. The author was unknown, the region ugly, but I was soon convinced of the book's truth and power. While it was a trifle too meticulous in the statement of its facts, and its values were too evenly distributed, it nevertheless appealed to me as the best picture of pioneer Illinois life yet written. It was less fantastic than Eggleston, and its characters were wholly unrelated to Dickens or any other writer. Its style, curiously spritely, was equally unconventional, and the speech of its chief character, "Zury, the meanest man in Spring County," phonetically exact. . . .[9]

Mentioning the correspondence between himself and Kirkland, Garland said that on May 31, 1887, Kirkland had sent him a copy of the novel in which he had made some revisions in order "to relieve my beloved Anne from any suspicions of wantonness such as (to my surprise) I find some women harboring against her."[10] Furthermore, Garland wrote, Kirkland asked him to give the amended copy to William Dean Howells for review.

Of his memories of Kirkland and their conversation, Garland wrote:

> The author of "Zury" was a small man, alert and humorous, with keen, black eyes and thick, dark eyebrows, and his home, a four-story mansion on the north side of the Chicago River, still further subdued me. He received me in his ground-floor study with cordial interest and after thanking me for my review of his novel, he began to quiz me.
>
> Briefly (I was too sick to be verbose) I gave him a history of my life while he leaned back in his chair and smilingly regarded me. He could hardly restrain his laughter, and yet I was the *Transcript* reviewer of his novel and his fine eyes grew sympathetic as I confessed that I had been two nights

in a day coach with only such sleep as a hard seat permitted, and then, remembering my mission, I turned interrogator. "How did you come to write 'Zury'?"

He explained that he had lived almost all his life in Illinois, part of the time in a small town. "I am the son of a pioneer woman writer, Caroline Kirkland," he said, "and I know farm life. All the characters in 'Zury' have their prototypes in my down-state acquaintances. The book is as true as I could make it. Many of its incidents are literally exact."[11]

Kirkland asked Garland why he did not write fiction; and, when Garland replied that he could not handle dialogue, Kirkland told him he was merely lazy. "You are the first actual farmer in literature," he said,[12] and Garland was impressed; in fact, he left Kirkland with the feeling that the author of *Zury* had opened a whole world of literary effort for him. On the way East, Garland stopped to see Kirkland again; he then told Kirkland that he hoped to write fiction and that, if he should become a successful writer of fiction, it would be the result of Kirkland's influence.

After Garland left the Kirkland house, Joseph sat down to write the details of the visit to his family. He reported that Garland had spent Saturday night and the forenoon on Sunday with him. He thought Garland "a country boy—farmer's son—largely self-educated . . ." who wanted to reform all literature by reconstructing it on a realistic basis. Kirkland noted that Garland urged him to devote himself entirely to literature, "even at the sacrifice of business."[13] Though Kirkland was for a time somewhat patronizing in his tone, he continued to correspond with Garland.

He wrote that he was delighted to know that some of Garland's friends were interested in *Zury*, that it pleased him to know that Hurd felt that it was dramatic, but that he could not see any dramatic quality in the book. "The *character* is rather picturesque but his life is utterly unstagey, to my thinking," he wrote. Moreover, when Garland suggested that *Zury* be made into a play, Kirkland doubted that it could be done. "Let's see—four acts—the hardening sufferings of youth—the rude and grotesque features of his prosperity—the grievous awakening on being refused by his lady love—the reformed and humanized gentleman. No—I can't see it. Undramatic in every line," he declared.[14]

Garland continued to suggest that the novel be made into a play, but Kirkland insisted that he give up the idea. He was certain no one would produce it. Kirkland finally suggested, however, that he would like to have *Zury* dramatized if he could go over the play after it had been written.[15] But he was more interested in the reception of the novel as shown by the reviews which appeared in some of the magazines of the day.

Early in July he had written to his wife that he thought that the novel would be well received, for one of his friends in Chicago, Judge Blodgett, had told him that the characters were like real people; Kirkland added that he had not been able to find any reviews of the novel in the magazines, but he expected to see them soon.[16] On July 25 he found a review in the *Nation,* and he wrote to his wife that *Zury* was "favorably reviewed," though the writer thought that the work lacked a strong plot to hold it together.[17] *The Critic* pointed out that the book was a fine piece of realism and welcomed Kirkland as a new writer who might develop into one of the major figures of the times.[18] The *Dial* stressed the realism of the book,[19] and the *Overland Monthly* contrasted Kirkland's lifelike characters with the drab manipulated ones of other writers—especially with those of Howe and Eggleston.[20]

William Dean Howells, who did not review the work in *Harper's Monthly Magazine* until June, 1888, thought that the work was a worth-while piece of realistic writing and that Kirkland was the first writer to put into fiction the western pioneer farmer whose aim in life was making money. He added that personal knowledge alone "does not suffice in such a case, and we are glad of an artist with clear eyes and an honest hand in the author of *Zury*—one incapable of painting life other than he had found it."[21] Undoubtedly Howells used the amended copy of the novel which Kirkland had asked Garland to give to him, for Kirkland was so concerned with the misunderstanding of the character of Anne that he had decided almost at once to revise the novel.

Believing that he must make changes in the work because

some reviewers felt that he had gone beyond propriety in the handling of sex, Kirkland quickly persuaded his publishers to bring out a second edition in which he could make some concessions to the public taste. By July, 1887, he had completed such revision as he then thought necessary, but he continued for some time to think about other possible revisions. He had reworked the novel very slightly to make Anne Sparrow into a somewhat sentimental female who clings to Zury Prouder for protection in the traditional romantic manner. Kirkland thought of taking out chapters five and twenty, but the publishers again refused to allow such major changes, and *Zury* remained as it had been printed in the second edition. The second edition of two hundred and seventy copies was published in December, 1887. Another printing was made in January, 1889, and still another in April, 1892.

In the second edition Kirkland inserted a preface which he hoped would make his intent clear. He wrote: "If a critic shall say—'This novel is a palpable imitation of Thomas Hardy's *Far From the Madding Crowd;* an attempt to reproduce, on American soil, the unflinching realism of the picture, given by that remarkable work, of English low life down in actual contact with the soil itself,—'

"Then the writer will be satisfied. He will know that he has hit his mark, or at least come near enough to it to make his aim evident."[22]

Kirkland hoped that he had created a novel in which character and setting would interact in such a way that every reader would be aware of the realism of each. He had used his characters to bring the scene into focus, and the scene to create character, and he had used whatever methods had come to hand for the purpose.

III   *Methods of Narration*

Kirkland's technique is not consistent. He does not maintain a single point of view; he slips from one character to another; and he intrudes for editorial comment. He reveals the story through a series of episodes on a roughly chronological plan. The episodes are not necessarily connected with each other except that they involve the same characters; but the characters are shown to grow, both in age and in complexity, through the episodes which are frequently though loosely constructed in the manner of the tall tale.

Kirkland had become aware of the humor and the dialect of the country folk of Illinois, in the addresses of Lincoln, and in the newspapers of the day. He examined the dialect to get veracity and raciness in his episodes; and he sought to provide social history—analytical, descriptive, and serious—through the development of his characters in the setting of Illinois farm and village life. He used the biographical anecdote—one of the staple techniques of humor—to provide not only character revelation and growth but also the verisimilitude he sought. And, with these awarenesses and his heritage from his mother, he built his tales and incidents around specific settings drawn from his memory.

The Wayback of *Zury* is one such specific setting; a frontier village, it is similar to the Pinckney of Kirkland's youth:

> . . . a cluster of houses surrounding the gristmill and sawmill on the river-bank. The few buildings were new, middle-aged, and old, as indicated by the various degrees of fading which they had undergone—green lumber, seasoned lumber, and grey, weather-beaten boards reduced almost to the color of the air that has desiccated them. They glared under the pitiless sunshine, asking in vain for the shadows of trees which had been on the ground before any houses intruded, but which had been unwisely sacrificed, leaving only ugly stumps to show where they had stood (p. 123).

As has been noted in Chapter One, the Kirklands had laid out their town in Michigan by a mill site and Caroline had fought unsuccessfully to keep the magnificent elm trees which adorned the town square. But the settlers had cut them down, and the ugly rotting stumps were reminders of their folly in the hot summer days which were to come. Joseph Kirkland remembered; and he intended in his novel to portray life as honestly as his own experiences reflected it.

But, at the same time, he hoped to make his novel truly universal in its purpose. His objective, as he announced it, is noble; it follows in a rough manner the great quest myth-cycle of human existence with its suffering and courage; with its endurance and reward for those who endure; and with its dark moments for those who are slain, for those who can not fight, and for those who are too weak to survive the hardships of the environment. But Kirkland changes the pace of the work too often; he forces too many series of events into limited space as he tries to focus his scenes and characters and description and speech; and, in his attempt to produce art, his method is often indirect rather than direct.

He tries to build action and character indirectly by employing environment and the work of men to form the basic ritual of life. His was not an unconscious usage, for he adapted for *Zury* his earlier observations from the description of farm life which he had written for *The Prairie Chicken*. In *Zury*, he wrote:

> "Breakin' " is the spring plowing; March and April, when the frost is out and the ground dry enough to turn over without being made "cloddy." "Plantin' " should begin about May first. "Corn-up" will follow in about ten days. "Wunst through," the completion of the first corn plowing, should be early June. "Laid by" will follow six or eight weeks later, some time in July. "Tosslin'," when the tassels begin to turn the field from green to yellow, will be before the beginning of August. "Corn-in-the-milk," by the middle, and "Ros'n ear," when the milk has coagulated into glutten and the ear may be roasted for the table—say by about September first. "Stockin'," butting up and placing in "shock" such portion as is kept for the sake of the fodder in stalks and leaves, takes October, and "getherin' " goes on all winter (pp. 55-56).

Thus the entire year is set out in colloquial terms of farm life: the ritual of life is narrowed by the single vital crop of the prairie farmers of Illinois, and the barren life of the people is ruled by its tillage of the soil. The episodes, connected slightly and by characters only, take on a living pattern as Kirkland moves toward localism in his study of environment and character; and the tale, always a part of the pioneer mode in America, becomes, in his hand, a type of communication which reveals the base of native life and character. Often, indeed, the episodes as well as the characters almost represent the forces of the social situation, moving toward symbols and parallels in which the human mind naturally works.

In his own way, however crudely, Kirkland tried to combine two of the most important traditions of American literature: one of psychological horror and the other of frontier humor and realism. The first Kirkland employs to explain character and the effect of environment on it; the second he uses to show the quality of life and to explain the comic sense which is so essentially a part of the whole scope of realism. Though he could not fuse the two into an unmistakable whole, as did Mark Twain, he did seize the essential native traditions in Illinois and preserve them as he pictured the pioneer against the local scene. He tried, with limited powers, to reach for the portrayal of the American against his background in a tradition which was still—for Kirkland—deeply imprinted with the pioneer spirit. Within that pioneer spirit, from his memory and with the hope of preserving something of the past which he himself had known, he drew scenes of realistic, primitive life; and he singled out the archetypal figure of Zury Prouder to commemorate. He used, therefore, the episode to embed more than one tale in order to create a longer form of fiction in which his store of social knowledge created the solid tradition of realistic fact. He wanted to do more than give a mere fragment of knowledge of life in early Illinois; and he used dialect, atmosphere, and prototypes for his work in order to give a sense of life to his creation.

He found, however, that the use of material from the past required that he use the flash-back in order to explain the present; and his use of it is often managed by means of a comic story which is told to illuminate an incident, a character, or a social custom. Indeed, Kirkland, like Zury Prouder himself, gloried in what he considers to be the tall tale for it is typically American fun to him. He used it in his flash-backs to turn the laughter into bitterness and disillusionment, but he often dispelled the bitterness he had created by portraying "smiling aspects" of life as it evolved on the prairie. This method is also closely associated with his style, for revelation is often accomplished by means of it rather than by structure.

Kirkland intended his use of episode to illustrate the theory of social stages in frontier society, and he portrayed the layers of the society in dialect and comic story. He also used his characters to demonstrate the rise through the layers of society, and he tried to keep his theories disguised by his art. He pointed out to Garland in one of his letters that he expected to conceal all his social study in art, for he felt that art somehow carried a stronger impact than did direct statement; yet he was careful to intrude for direct editorializing at any point where he wished to stress idea. He tried, however, to portray his ideas through the rise of Zury Prouder in the society of Illinois as well as in the rise in sensibility, and he employed the change in the Prouder house from a typical weather-beaten, unattractive farmhouse to a well-kept, landscaped, modern house to state his ideas and to symbolize them. The method he used to show the rise of his central character is a combination of structure, style, development of character itself, and plot on two levels; and all these must be juxtaposed as Kirkland intended if his creation is to be realized in all its strength.

IV Plot

Plot did not come easily to Kirkland because he saw life in terms of incident or episode; and, though he wanted complications, he had difficulty selecting precisely those episodes which would cross and recross without giving the impression of artificiality. His material, because he wanted to be objective, was not easily handled, and he could not, like Henry James, trace out the larger pattern in the details of a segment; but he did hit on his characters as the principal means of holding his novel together; and his characters, though true to life as he embroiled them in action, sometimes produce the impression that the action itself is artificially contrived. Indeed, were it not for the psychology of his characters and the reality of his settings, we should dismiss his plots as mere arrangements not dissimilar to the popular romances which he, along with Howells and other realists, so soundly condemned.

The arrangement is detailed by Kirkland in the opening paragraph of the last chapter of *Zury*: "We picked up our homespun thread at the Prouder section: we followed it in its windings, knots, and twists to the school, the woods-fire, the riot, the stump, the polls, the machine shop, the mines, and many scenes beside. Now, a whole generation later (well on in 'the Fifties'), it leads us back to the very place we started from" (p. 509). The arrangement he suggests is like a circle made of thread or rope, full of knots, twists, and loops; and his episodes are the knots, twists, and loops of the rope.

In the circular arrangement Kirkland was not always careful to provide sufficient motivation for all action. When John McVey disappears into California to die of fever, the action is not convincing; but, since Kirkland no longer has use for him, he disposes of him in the quickest way possible. Furthermore, Kirkland can not bear to continue the story with Zury Prouder remaining unflinchingly a "business is business" man, and the softening of his character is done in a far too romantic fashion—the true love of Anne Sparrow McVey brings about his change. In mellowing the character of Zury, Kirkland telescoped too much material; the reader feels that the transformation needs to be explained in other terms, that the author had suddenly realized he must end the novel, and that he does so in the most convenient way. For the plot does not work itself out as a well-constructed one should: there is no center; there is no major decision worked out in clear design; Kirkland's characters do move around, but there is no clear line of movement from one thing to another. The plot is in no way symmetrical, and it is imposed on the characters in such a way that it is often trivial. Kirkland seems at times to have been ruled by his material as much as he ruled it; and he could not master the craftsmanship which marked the novels of his greater contemporaries.

Nevertheless, Kirkland does have plausibility in his local color and therefore in the life of his people. Although the contrivance of some of the situations shows the ingenuity rather than the art of Kirkland, the novel does somehow bring Zury Prouder from poverty, bitterness, and unhappiness to success as a rich, respected farmer who reaps the reward of happiness for having endured the suffering of learning from life itself.

V *Style*

Kirkland's style is dominated by the use of dialect—a device for creating his characters as well as illustrating the social scene. He attempted in his novel to create and to give life to his men and women through the most careful phonetic notation he was capable of, through elliptical syntax, through the omission of unemphatic words in their speech, and through figurative diction drawn from the farms and the country stores.

Kirkland uses exact terms which he included in a glossary at the end of *Zury* for the use of those who might not understand his colloquialisms. "Nary," "niggering logs," "snaking logs," "takin' stock," "talkin' turkey," "humbly"—these add to the reality of his dialogue and to his people. The dialogue reflects the characters. Old Anstey says to Anne Sparrow when he meets her after the school board examination: "Wal, I'llaowed t'take ye t'our'us ef so be ye c'd put up with poor folk's doin's over-night. I jest went hum 'n' raouted aout the'ole woman 'n' told her her 'n' me we'd take a shake-down up garret so's ye c'd hev a night's rest—ye look t'need it—traveled so fur, 'n' had sech bad luck wi'yer'zam'nation 'n' all!" (pp. 102-3).

The mixture of ellipsis in syntax and words work their spell, as Kirkland well knew, for he explained his method in a letter to Garland: "if this lingo—now spoken by some ten millions of people—is to be crystallized: it must be done by taking an average and *sticking to it*. It is a composite photograph, establishing a type. I took it (modified, of course) from the country district in Central Illinois where I spent ten years and whence I drew my subject."[23] He points out that he renders "this here" as "this h'yer," "talking about canoeing" as "talkin' 'baout canoe-in'"; and he indicated his use of compressed syllables and figures of speech in such terms as "a mild o' fence, pig-tight, bull-strong 'n' hoss-high." He admits that he has seen the use of some of his speech and humor in a Chicago paper, and he had been much pleased.

But Kirkland did not rely upon dialect entirely, for he drew his descriptive scenes with an economy equal to that of the speech of his characters. The hardships of the Prouder family during their first year on the prairie are reflected in Kirk-land's terse prose:

> They did break a little prairie that season, though it was too
> late to put in any crop. They called it twelve acres, but it
> wasn't. They thought they could get it fenced before frost,
> but they couldn't. They hoped for a mild winter, but it proved
> a severe one; for several years afterwards it was remembered,
> and in bitter jest styled "the year eighteen-hundred-and-froze-
> to-death." They felt almost sure of sustaining their beasts
> till the spring grass should start, but one of the mares died.
> They resolved not to mortgage any of their land, but they
> were disappointed (p. 27).

The bitterness both of the winter and of emotion is detailed
in the understatement which describes the death of the little
Prouder girl:

> It was this way: The little girl, who might have lived, and
> even thriven, in a warm, rich and comfortable city home,
> could not bear the cruelty of her environments, and died
> after long, quiet suffering. . . . Ephraim had fallen asleep
> by the fire, and Zury had fled out into the pitiless snow-
> storm—the black fury in his heart outvieing the white blast
> about his head. At last Selina laid her hand on her husband's
> shoulder. . . . He called Zury in from the path . . . and both
> men sat by the fireside till morning, while Selina straighted
> the wasted limbs, put on the poor girl's best clothes, tied up
> the sharp chin and closed the eyes with—something. They had
> no coins to lay on the lids (p. 28).

The cruelty of the elements, the poverty of the family, and
the silent suffering are sketched swiftly and with simplicity:

> Nobody could reach them through the pathless snow. There
> was not even a burial until spring thawed the ground so that
> a grave could be dug. Ephraim tried it, but it was like pick-
> ing at a bed of sandstone. Then Zury cleared the snow off
> a little space, and built there a huge fire, to soften the obdurate
> bosom of mother earth, hardened against thus untimely re-
> ceiving her own . . . when day broke there was only a fresh
> white drift where the fire had been. Then they fixed two
> crotched sticks against the back of the house, and set the

little coffin on them, where it remained until April came, and with it a day sufficiently humane to allow death the rights which even death possesses (p. 29).

In his simple style, with taciturn intensity, Kirkland is at his best. He creates the atmosphere of the blackest hour of Zury's boyhood with it, but he turns to contrast in an almost romantic and gothic mood when he creates the atmosphere of the summer on the prairie:

> Summer night—unless fear distort the vision—is beautiful, but summer morning in the malarial regions (to the experienced dweller) is positively ugly. All night the world is a lovely, half veiled Danae: with break of day she becomes a squalid, unkempt, disorderly invalid. A blue, unwholesome-looking haze spreads over every flat space, and the rays of dawn silver its surface with a pale, sickly light. Ague, like the ghost of a giant snake, crawls visible over the land: men shudder at the sight, and their flesh creeps at its very hideousness (p. 106).

Kirkland varies his style, going from the dialect of his low characters to the quasi-literary—classical allusion and metaphor and simile. Yet the style is not intended to be a device for itself alone; it is the means of giving life to his characters and to his settings in his attempt to present the reality of life as he saw and knew it.

VI *Character*

In *Zury* Kirkland built a picture of life; and the novel centers around the character of Zury Prouder whom he modeled from life. For his portrait he used Usual H. and John Meeker, father and son, who had come to the Middle West in the days following the War of 1812.[24] Usual H. Meeker had taken up land in Fountain County, Indiana, where he and his son John had become known for hard work, sharp practices, and a fortune of about two hundred thousand dollars. John, who moved away from the original homestead, spent his last days in Danville, Illinois, at the home of his daughter whom Kirkland knew. Kirkland, therefore, knew not only the story of Usual Meeker's life and struggles but also his reputation which had grown through tall tales current in the vicinity of Danville and Tilton. Thus Joseph Kirkland, writing from his own knowledge, created his character in a manner which placed him in the main stream of realism in writing in his epoch. But above all, he built a picture of a man, one who is known as "mean" in the title of the novel but who is as real as any man can be.

Yet Zury Prouder is not "mean" in the usual sense of the word, for he is keenly appreciated by his acquaintances:

> Men liked to be with Zury and hear his gay shrewd talk; to trade with him, and meet his frankly brutal greed. He enjoyed popularity, and liked to do good turns to others when it cost him nothing. When elected to local posts of trust and confidence he served the public in the same efficient fashion in which he served himself, and he was therefore continually elected to school directorships and other "thank'ee jobs" (p. 87).

In his creation of the man Kirkland tried to see life with compassion but with detachment; he sought always that mysterious process which finds meaning in experience and turns it into literature in an attempt to give significance to the contradictions of life. Hence, he portrays Zury as not having been "mean" all his life: as a boy he is sensitive, affectionate, hard-working, inventive, and generous. Experience and grief turned him into something else.

The experience and dark grief brought by what seemed to be the unnecessary death of his little sister changed Zury; his

> grief was passionate and heart-rending . . . and after Zury's outburst of feeling he settled down into a stony hardness. Those tears for his "baby" sister were the last tears he shed for many a year. It was as if the fountain had filled up and run over a few drops, and then frozen solid. All this poverty, toil, distress, and the terrible need for money, made a deep impression on the forming mind of the youth; and being of a logical turn, he "put this and that together," and drew conclusions fitted to the premises as he saw them. Money was life; the absence of money was death. "All that a man hath will he give for his life"; *ergo* all that a man hath will he give for money (p. 30).

The acquisition of money becomes his central motive in life, and his purpose is fixed: "I'm goin' t' own a mortgage 'fore I die. . ." (p. 53). Nothing stands in his way: he is determined to be a "wholesaler all my life, or die a-trying" so that "he was without associates, ambitions, or objects in life, except in the first place 'subduing' that farm; in the next place, clearing it of mortgages; in the third place, increasing its money-making capacities; and thenceforth and forever adding dollar to dollar, mortgage to mortgage (on other people's farms), note to note, and gain to gain, with all the force of a strong intellect pent into a narrow channnel" (p. 65).

Yet Zury is admired by his neighbors because he is able to make money: "Th' ain't nothin' *mean* about Zury, mean's he is. Gimme a man as sez right aout 'look aout fer yerself,' 'n' I kin get along with him" (p. 86). For Zury's neighbors know that he is honest; he must stand alone and he knows that honesty is the best policy. All who know him are aware that "business is business" with him and that no emotional coloring will be permitted in any transaction which involves gain.

Zury remains the hard, cold trader until after the birth of twins to Anne McVey. As the twins grow up, he is attracted to them, especially to Phil the boy, who looks like his real father and who is a natural mechanic. Zury glories in Phil's ability and in his spunk; but, when he hears Phil repeat a tall tale about one of Zury's schemes to make money, he is ashamed. He does not want Phil to regard him as a schemer, and he tries to change.

The change becomes apparent to Anne, especially after Zury has served in the legislature. "His English was in a transition state. With attention he could express himself reasonably well, and this attention he habitually gave when talking with Anne and other educated persons" (p. 421). He tries to make himself into a better man in Anne's eyes; and, when she refuses to marry him, he blames himself, calling himself a fool, "low-down trash, Poor Ignor'nt old miser! Morgage-sharp, Land-shark!" (p. 441). As he tries desperately to change himself more, his neighbors are puzzled by his actions. Finally, when Anne accepts his proposal of marriage, his character is definitely mellowed; he has regained some

of his boyhood characteristics. Yet, his is a full-length portrait
—the first, complete figuration of a farmer in American fiction.

After Kirkland had built Zury into a successful dirt farmer,
he showed other phases of his life. The phase of greatest importance is the influence of Anne Sparrow McVey on him.
For she is the foil for Zury, the character of contrast. Kirkland
followed the idea that character should be explored to create
it, and he juxtaposed the two central characters—the unedu-
cated, crude man and the educated, liberated, clever girl.
Zury is narrow and provincial, but adaptable—Anne is slower
to adapt, but she helps the other to evolve. In creating the
character of Anne, Kirkland went further than was common
in the literature of the day, for he suggested that she is
liberal beyond most women of her era.

Anne was reared in Lowell, Massachusetts, by a mother
who was intellectual and literary but who was supported by
her daughter's wages from work in a cotton mill. Anne read
a good deal, tried her hand at writing, and held herself aloof;
for "she and her mother were above their business" (p. 91).
As she grew older, Anne realized that "no one whom she
would marry would ever offer himself" (p. 91), and she joined
a group of followers of Fourier, whose philosophy "aimed at
giving every human being an honorable chance to live; no
wonder it gained passionate adherents from the ranks of New
England women, Anne Sparrow among the rest" (p. 91).

When her mother died, Anne drifted into a group of "ad-
vanced thinkers"; and, under the guidance of a young doctor,
she became one of the "come-outers." Kirkland suggested
that the story and actions of such affairs among New England "socialists" may never be entirely told; and as "to Anne's
part in it we need not inquire how far from the beaten track
her 'broad views' led her. Whatever she did was not done
from Wickedness; it was in accordance with her honest
opinion of right and wrong, and not in violation of them"
(p. 92). Furthermore, Anne suffers from a flaw, "mental or
physical, it is hard to say which," a characteristic which
Kirkland indicates will affect her future. She is afraid of the
dark—with a sort of insanity "but it was no more to be conquered than is that of a poor lunatic who kills himself to
escape imaginary perils threatening his life" (p. 92). Her

terror can be conquered only by the presence of an older, stronger person; and she will go to any length to assure herself of the presence of such a person when she is terrorized.

Kirkland built Anne's fear of darkness purposefully and carefully. Shortly after she arrives in Wayback and is examined by the members of the school board, she is left alone in the dark. Her terror is made plain: "Once more her old well-known fear of being frightened fell upon her with a force greater than ever before. Her hair took on its horrid independent life and moved audibly and sensibly beneath her hat, and roughening chills shot over her body and limbs" (p. 101). The terror constricts her throat, and she has no control over herself.

The terror returns in the scene with which Kirkland built the turning of his romantic love plot. In the darkness, after the picnic and with the fire darting around her, Anne is not sure of what she sees: "Strange beasts and reptiles seem to be darting past her, fleeing from the fire" (p. 219). The terror increases; when she and Zury have reached the safety of the coal mine by the river bank, she will not allow him to leave her. Her insane cunning dictates her actions: "In her piteous plight she was suddenly seized with the boldness, the cunning, and the recklessness of desperation" (p. 222). She suggests to Zury that he would not leave her if they were married; and, when she clings to him, he mistakes her action for passion: "She was Anne Sparrow, and dark night was all around above, below, at right and left, before and behind her—Zury was the only object whereon her eyes could rest without a shudder. Insanity gibed and gibbered at her from all else. She took hold of his coat with both her hands, bowed her head upon them, and again sobbed aloud" (p. 253). Zury "took her in his arms and carried her over the fire to her rude couch, and did not try again to leave her" (p. 253).

The next morning Anne is no longer afraid; and later, when she discovers that she is pregnant, she accepts her responsibility. She appeals to Zury only because she has no money at all. For Anne is, as Kirkland points out, "more of a bohemian than what the polite world would call a well-bred, well ordered damsel" (p. 201). She seemed "a perfect woman nobly planned" by comparison with the women of the Illinois community, and Kirkland does not propose that she be thought of otherwise. He does not intend that she be regarded as wanton, and he altered her character in his revision of the novel when he found that some readers misinterpreted his intentions. He had aspired to be realistic, in so far as his talents would allow, but he had no intention of being coarse. By changing Anne's character, he weakened the novel and the character, for he made her into a clinging vine who followed the romantic tradition and who was taken advantage of as a result. But the realism remains, and even the revision does not destroy the validity of his treatment of life in early Illinois.

Kirkland had not intended to be immoral in his use of sex as a part of his characterization. He had gone further than most writers, practicing advice which William Dean Howells was to give later to Garland: the writer of realism should not neglect the sheer brute attraction of male and female. Kirkland had intended that his creation of a psychological flaw in Anne's character should make her blameless. But even so, he was in advance of his time, as Benjamin Lease has pointed out;[25] for he was one of the writers who laid the basis for the present frank treatment of sex in literature.

Most writers of the times had not gone so far as Kirkland: Howells, James, and Mark Twain had not dared to do so.[26] They had employed the kiss or the embrace as a useful literary convention and as a substitute for sex, and Howells had remarked specifically about "palpitating divans." For though the writers of Kirkland's day knew that man's brute instinct for woman must be admitted to literature in the future, they knew that conventions served their own purposes better than photographic descriptions which, in the long run, have proved to be more difficult to handle; for inevitably such descriptions border on mere pornography or the ridiculous. Certainly Kirkland would not have gone so far in his characterization of Anne Sparrow McVey had he known that he would be misunderstood in his intentions; for, as has been noted, when he discovered the temper of the public toward her, he conformed her character to the limitations of the times. He had only tried to show that character comes from nature and environment; but he was more successful, perhaps in the study of Zury or his minor characters than he was in the character of Anne.

Kirkland tried always to use the physical background as the setting for character, and the setting has a social and an economic order which is characterized by the ability of men to move from one rank to another with the flexibility and fluidity of the newly settled frontier. The manners and customs have been crystallized by the environment, but the social stages have been set by the economic growth of the citizens.

The humble characters, typified by the Ansteys, point up the social and economic factors. Handled in a playful manner, they provide comic relief from the more somber characters. They serve to give the opportunities for amusement, for humor, for the tall tales which reveal Zury's character, and for the tenderness which Kirkland needed to establish the lifelike quality of his novel. These people—resigned to their own inadequacies and worn out with ague—provide also the means for the demonstration of social stages, of economic realism, of psychology, and of the concept of environment as a creative influence in determining character. They show the set ways of custom and the dumb wonder of the totally ignorant; and they provide a foil for the sharpness of Zury, who responds to the necessities of life and who demonstrates social growth and cultural awareness as he comes under the influence of Anne Sparrow.

The obscurity of the people who surround Zury does not keep them from the decidedly proficient use of humor to illustrate their points or to give weight to their criticisms of everything which their narrow circle encompasses. They suggest their limitation of conversational subjects, and Kirkland uses them to suggest what he could not picture directly to his reader. These people have all the awkwardness, the loneliness, and the suffering of their limitations; but they respond to kindliness. They are submissive to what they consider to be fate, and they note briefly what might have been. They play the chorus to the main action and to the main characters who are sharpened by their comments and by contrast with them. They carry the story by episode, and they add to the contrived complications which Kirkland sought in his parade of incident. Their speech—the dialect—is real, elided, nasal, true to the ear—the result of Kirkland's careful observations and notations, which, even as a boy, he learned should demand the attention of a realist if he wanted to reveal society through its language.

Kirkland followed in other ways the creed of the realist in his characterization; like Howells or Henry James he knew that character often determines action and that action determines character; and he made his characters more important than his plot as he wrote of the commonplace. But he pointed also toward idealism and noted somewhat that the realism of his characters and setting is but the expression of a quickly growing democracy. He showed his belief that the average human being can, by the exertion of his will, become unusual; that man is not placed in a predestined universe in which his will can not prevail. And, though he studied men and women in their environment and though he made a "social study," he was optimistic in his attitude; for he believed that continuity, process, struggle, environment, and the evolutionary concept of social progress are the tools for the interpretation of the life of his people. He demonstrated that he believed that much of the confusion of his day resulted from having made man the satellite of the external instead of placing him, as he deserved to be placed, in the position of central sway. He studied, therefore, each of his characters in relation to the society in which he is placed.

Each of Kirkland's characters becomes a social study in miniature of the evolution of character because of the inevitable influence of the social circle in which he moves. In turn, by example, the two most developed characters exert influence which helps the less fortunate members of the immediate community to achieve a realization that life is not composed of the small circle of land on which they eke out a living, that there are comforts to be purchased with money, that there is responsibility to society, and that man has the possibility of growth in social and cultural awareness. Kirkland also showed his belief in man's ability to develop because of religion, and his interest may have been sharpened by the religious differences in his own family background.

Kirkland's parents had been Unitarians; but his father had had some difficulty in deciding to leave the Congregationalism of the Kirkland family, and he had finally decided to leave Hamilton College because he could not agree with its religious policies. The Kirklands had long been New England in religious affiliation, for Samuel Kirkland had been a missionary to the Indians in New York, and the land which was granted to him for his work in the Revolutionary War became the basis for the establishment of Hamilton College. Too, coming as they had from Maine, the Kirklands had followed the dominant strain of Puritanism in the earlier days, for they were descended from a Joseph Kirkland and a Sallie Backus, the latter being a descendant of William Bradford of Plymouth Plantation fame, and they followed in the tradition of training for service to the community. John Thornton Kirkland, son of the founder of Hamilton College, became the president of Harvard College; and General Joseph Kirkland, grandfather of the author of *Zury*, not only served in the Revolutionary War but followed his brother to New York State to become the first mayor of Utica. In the Kirkland family, religion was regarded soberly and was the basis of public service. The Kirklands did their duty as they saw it.

Joseph's mother, Caroline Stansbury Kirkland, was the descendant of a notable family of royalist principles, and her grandfather, Joseph Stansbury, had been one of the Tory poets of the Revolution. He had fled to Canada, but later returned to his business in Philadelphia and New York. He had married Sara Ogier, a French Huguenot, and his son Samuel had married Elizabeth Alexander of New Jersey. Caroline Stansbury, their daughter, was reared principally in New York City where her father ran a book store, though she went to the school of her aunt who ran a private school for girls at Utica. Caroline's brother Joseph had accepted English citizenship and the Anglican Church in order to inherit a fortune left to him by a member of the Stansbury family. Religion in the Stansbury family was almost a matter of social standing, and it was not a matter of much concern otherwise; but Caroline was always interested in the moral quality of any society in which she lived.

Because of his family background, it was natural, then, that Kirkland should be interested in religion as it appeared among the settlers of Illinois and that he used it as material to help delineate character and the society of which he wrote.

In *Zury* he introduced the "little sect of Christians called 'Soul-sleepers,' from their individual guess as to the fate of mankind between death and judgment," a sect to which Zury's father belongs. The sect, he noted, had founded a college in Ohio, an act of suicide, for when "you educate a Soul-sleeper he ceases to be one" (p. 66). Yet Zury looks with longing to that college as a possible way for him to find a life which he vaguely feels might provide him with a ship on "the sea of knowledge, of which he had learned so little," and which he desires when he has time to think of himself—though he has precious little time for anything but work in the early years.

But when Zury discovers that his father's superstition has been fanned into cupidity, and the cupidity into liberality so that he has promised a sum of money to the college, Zury loses interest in the college, in the religion, and in everything except a way to keep the money. In the end, his father, derided by Zury, simply tears up his agreement, and the way out of his pledge is found. Zury, who has done with religion, is regarded by his neighbors as "unsaved." Later, when he is accused of being a Universalist because papers of that sect are found in his barn, he is made acceptable to the community by his explanation that the papers were packing for his new windmill. The neighbors quickly decide to buy no more windmills from a company which tolerates such religious views. When Anne Sparrow hears the story from Mr. Anstey, she quickly concludes that liberal thought in religion will not be tolerated in a community where public confession of sin and an obvious emotional experience of rebirth are necessary to demonstrate that one is of the elect.

Kirkland portrayed the same sort of community in *The McVeys*. Phil, induced to go to one of the meetings of a religious group, is impressed with the idea that the ranting, fainting, and general hysteria are like those of an asylum of lunatics—but, he notes, voluntary ones. Kirkland hints at the psychological basis of escape from frustration which is a part of the manifestation, and he makes Phil into a man who has no concern with religion. It is true that Phil falls in love with Anne Marsten, the daughter of a preacher, but the Marstens are comfortably settled and their religion has a more settled, genteel tone. It is this tone of the genteel religion which Kirkland uses in some of the characterizations in *The Captain of Company K.*

William Faregon, the hero of *The Captain of Company K,* is a successful man, a teacher of a Sunday School class, and an organizer of religion in his church, one of the popular society churches of Chicago. Furthermore, Sara Penrose, Faregon's sweetheart, is the daughter of a minister not at all unlike Preacher Marsten grown more well off and popular; and the church, the Sabbath, and Sunday as symbols of respectability are much in the conversation. The church is distinctly a social institution, a place of conformity and pleasure for the well-mannered congregation. Thus Kirkland demonstrates the growth of social stages through his use of religion and the church as part of the development of his characters. The reader feels at times that, like his mother, he often deliberately became "decidedly low"—stooped down to his characters and his settings; but he helped them to rise, socially and morally, by putting them through stages of evolution in his society.

VII *Theme and Importance*

Although much crudity and uncertainty characterize the technique of Kirkland's *Zury,* there is no uncertainty in its theme. Kirkland stated it clearly in the opening paragraph:

> Great are the toils and terrible the hardships that go to the building up of a frontier farm; inconceivable to those who have not done the task or watched its doing. In the prairies, Nature has stored, and preserved thus far through the ages, more life-materials than she ever before amassed in the same space. It is all for man, but only for such men as can take it by courage and hold it by endurance. Many assailants are slain, many give up and fly, but he who is sufficiently brave, and strong, and faithful, and fortunate, to maintain the fight to the end, has his ample reward (p. 1).

The novel carries out the theme: Zury Prouder is brave, strong, faithful, fortunate; and he has his ample reward.

Kirkland's faithfulness to reality helped him use the primitive force of nature to create real people; and, though his weak men fall in the battle with the forces, his strong win the fight to control their own destinies. Kirkland pleads for charity, for understanding, for the repudiation of narrow traditional practices which turn truth and reality into falsehood and hypocrisy for the sake of appearance. He pleads for the sympathetic human heart, for the hand of brotherhood given freely to suffering men and women; and, in the final analysis, he pleads for simple endurance in the battle to conquer the material world in the reach toward spiritual freedom.

Zury, though not a great book, is a good one; it is one of the first stories of the western farmer; and it has, as Vernon Louis Parrington pointed out, a secure place in the history of American fiction.[27] A work of considerable power, it led the way for other writers of novels of the Midwest and it delineated a character which John T. Flannigan says is as good for detailing the passion for wealth as Scott Fitzgerald's work is for symbolizing the jazz age.[28] The importance of the novel has been testified to by Lloyd Lewis,[29] Dorothy Dondore,[30] Lucy Lockwood,[31] Arthur H. Quinn,[32] Carl Van Doren,[33] Alexander Cowie,[34] and by Henry Nash Smith in his article in *The Literary History of the United States* (1948)[35] and in *The Virgin Land*.[36] Alfred Kazin has treated *Zury* as one of the novels of primitive realism which laid the groundwork for the present mature and healthy literature of the United States,[37] and Bernard Duffy has pointed to the solid quality of the novel.[38]

Certainly there can be little doubt that *Zury* sets down the life of the Middle West in all its crudeness—the constriction of pioneer life with its harshness and waste of finer values, the rude surroundings which limit the characters, and the struggle for survival are clearly set forth. Yet Kirkland has given the final triumph to man, for the very struggle in which his people engage gives dignity to them and reality to his fiction.

CHAPTER 6

The McVeys and The Captain of Company K

N O SOONER had Kirkland finished his first novel than he began to write *The McVeys*. He finished much of it by July, 1887, but it required steady work. Every night he wrote a few pages, reporting his progress to his family in Michigan. On June 17, 1887, he wrote to his daughter Caroline that he had finished twenty pages the night before,[1] and he wrote again on June 20 to say that he had written thirty more pages.[2] But in a letter of June 22 he reported that he had run into difficulties because he had used up his small store of local color in the writing of *Zury*.[3] On July 2 he wrote to his sister-in-law, Dorothy Wilkinson, that the story made slow progress,[4] but a few days later he wrote to his daughter Louise that he had finished a whole chapter.

No day without some lines was Kirkland's creed, and he followed it faithfully. But the novel went slowly, for "Zury the great hung like a cloud over future success."[5] Although he feared that the new novel would not be equal to *Zury*, he liked it better. "The book," he wrote to Garland on February 13, 1888, "has less rugged strength than *Zury;* its subject deals with mild village life instead of grim farm life; it has far less dialect; it has more fun, more romance, more sweetness; it has at least *one* more carefully studied character than any in *Zury;* it has Zury and Anne and Phil and Meg, besides a little bevy of new people."[6]

By March, 1888, Houghton,. Mifflin and Company had informed Kirkland that they would publish the novel, but he did not like the terms. He wrote to Garland to ask him to read the novel, to show it to anyone whom he wished to see it, and to advise him about the possible revisions.[7] On March 20, 1888, he wrote again to Garland, saying that he had started a war novel;[8] but on March 28 he wrote that he thought he might revise *The McVeys* by deleting the whole of Chapter 28, the story of Zury's $1000 Blunder, the business of the railroad, the letter about a singing school, the story of Dolly's baby—he was afraid his use of sex would again be misunderstood—and any other part of the novel which Garland might blue-pencil. He hoped to leave Chapter 16, "The Revival," for he thought that it illustrated some of his ideas of growth in social stages and that would not offend any readers.[9]

He had already done much revision at the request of Houghton, Mifflin and Company, and he had experimented with some of the material which he had sold as a short story to *Ehrich's Monthly Magazine* where it appeared in October, 1887. By May, 1888, he had sent the revised work to the publishers, and he waited eagerly to see if his second novel would be received as well as his first.

I *Narrative, Method, and Reception*

Kirkland opened *The McVeys* with a summary view of Zury, "now the meanest man in Spring County," but who, he forecasts, will "become possessed of a heart and soul fairly typical of the great and generous West in its ideal development."[10] In summarizing the character of Anne Mc-Vey, Kirkland indicated that the beginning of his novel was in the 1840's, and he presented her as a widow living in Springville who maintained herself and her twins by keeping books in a wholesale feed store. Meg, the girl, has become interested in writing, and she spends much of her time thinking about becoming owner of the *Springville Bugle*. Phil, the boy, is a mechanic of great ability.

By chapter three, Kirkland brings the twins into their teens, and he introduces one of the main characters, Dr. Stafford, through an incident in which Phil fractures his leg while trying to work out a mechanical method of running grindstones. Formerly, Dr. Stafford had been a sailor, and Kirkland used knowledge gained during his years at sea to draw his picture of the doctor's experience. After Phil's recovery, the doctor teaches him surveying, and together the two help lay out the route of the Galena and Chicago Railroad. During the work, Phil meets the girl Dolly, who later becomes the wife of Jim Sanders, a storekeeper who gives up his business to become an engineer on the railroad.

Kirkland returns to Zury to tell of his election to the legislature, and he introduces Judge David Davis, Stephen Douglas, and even Abraham Lincoln into the story when the last-mentioned brings the Circuit Court to Springville. Kirkland portrays Lincoln as a good lawyer and as one who remembers Zury for having rescued a Negro, an incident from the first novel. Kirkland also introduces Lincoln as the defender of a man known as "B'God Hobbs," a dark, twisted, vicious character, who is also the stepfather of Dolly Sanders. As time passes, Dr. Stafford falls in love with Anne, asks her to marry him, and is rejected.

The doctor takes Phil under his wing and helps the boy get started with the railroad, and Phil eventually becomes the engineer of *The Pioneer,* one of the famous engines of the Galena and Chicago Railroad. Meg becomes a writer for the *Bugle;* and she finds that, after Zury visits the family, her writing improves because she uses the strong imagery which has always marked Zury's speech.

Phil's total lack of interest in religion is portrayed by Kirkland in a scene in which Phil refuses to conform to village custom. Eventually Phil leaves Springville to live in Chicago where he rooms with Jim and Dolly Sanders. He becomes infatuated with Dolly who is a tease determined to capture Phil, but he escapes from her when he meets and falls in love with Ann Marsten, the daughter of one of his mother's former pupils. Kirkland causes Perry Fenton, a Chicago merchant, to fall in love with the girl also, but the two men, though rivals in love, become close friends.

Zury, in the meantime, has planned for Phil's future by buying a lead mine in Galena; he hopes Phil will become its manager. But Phil has angered B'God Hobbs, and he is fatally injured in a railroad accident which Hobbs causes. Hobbs is lynched by a mob, but Zury is desolate. He is able to get to Phil before the boy dies, and he expresses his grief in terms of David mourning for Absalom. When he reveals that Phil is his son, Phil calls him "daddy" and dies. This sentimentality almost wrecks the novel.

Phil's death brings Anne and Zury together, and they plan to be married. After the wedding, they go on a tour to New Orleans, to Pittsburgh, to Washington, and back to the Prouder farm. Zury has had the house remodeled, and he and Anne settle down to a happy life. The happy life is detailed in the last chapter of *Zury* as well as in *The McVeys*. Meg, who has refused to marry Dr. Stafford, continues to be happy in Springville where Zury's generosity has helped her purchase the *Springville Bugle*. The novel tells the story of the events between the last two chapters of *Zury* and is properly called *The McVeys: An Episode*.

The novel did not appear until September, 1888, and Kirkland, on a trip to Pendleton, Idaho, for the Caribou Mining Company, was afraid that critics might not like it.[11] He was right in his appraisal, for most critics thought it too loose in structure and too episodic in nature. Howells, writing in *Harper's Monthly Magazine*,[12] suggested that Kirkland was too close to his characters to see them clearly. The critic of the *Dial* suggested that Kirkland's realism was like Hardy's but his form was like Charles Reade's.[13] The *Atlantic Monthly* called attention to the lack of plot but noted the realistic pictures of small-town life.[14] The *Overland Monthly* praised the realism of the work and declared that the novel was really quite good because it lacked the sensationalism of works such as Howe's *Story of a Country Town*.[15]

As the critic of the *Atlantic Monthly* observed, Kirkland's second novel had little plot; but it also had other weaknesses. Because Kirkland had difficulty organizing *The McVeys*, he returned again and again to his first novel and repeated its episodes and incidents. Although he introduced real people and historical incidents to create a sense of reality, he also became more romantic and sentimental. Because he had to depict Zury as a "softened" character and because he had to make the work convincing, he found that he had to use incident and episode as he had in *Zury*. His episodes are strung on a thin thread of romance; he does attempt to foreshadow the death of Phil; and he does make his love plot less startlingly psychological than that of *Zury*. But the novel has no real plot; it depends upon the characters who appear and reappear to hold it together.

One obvious difference between the style of *Zury* and that of *The McVeys* lies in the employment of dialect. Kirkland consciously decreased the use of dialect in *The McVeys* because he was treating village life, and it represented a stage in social growth and, therefore, characters who were better educated than those of the farm. Although dialogue plays an important role in the revelation of character, the style becomes much more descriptive than that of *Zury*. Furthermore, as in *Zury*, Kirkland intrudes to editorialize or moralize throughout the novel. Although he knew that he was being romantic in both tone and episode and although he preferred his second novel to *Zury*, he failed in *The McVeys* to make effective use of his theories of realism in the treatment of anything but his characters. Although the novel does portray village life, it is too sweetly sentimental to merit classification with *Zury* as an example of rugged realism.

II *Characters of The McVeys*

The characters of *The McVeys* are more real than any other parts of the work. Zury, softened and seeking the hand of Anne McVey, is drawn with a sure if sentimental hand; Anne continues to be unusual. But Dr. Stafford is carefully studied as a physician, as a man in love—first with Anne and then with Meg—and as a learned, cultivated gentleman who holds no bitterness because he loses in love but, feeling that fate has played a comic trick on him, philosophizes about it.

Kirkland also paid close attention to the creation of other characters. Perry Fenton, a young man from Chicago who resembles the Kirkland of the 1850's, is proper and cultivated —inclined to gentleness and a love for literature. He is a churchgoer, especially because he feels the reforming influence of the church must be used in Chicago to help the poor; and he is drawn to Anne Marsten not only by her beauty but by the fact that her father is a minister. He is contrasted with Phil, who is portrayed as independent in mind and spirit. Dolly Sanders, the tease who tries to trap Phil, is shown first as a poor girl who has a kind of beauty and finally, when she flings herself at Phil, as a clearly immoral woman. Kirkland, bordering again on the brute attraction of male and female, tried to suggest reality; but he has Anne Marsten save Phil from the clutches of the wicked woman.

Kirkland hints that Phil has not always been saved by the love of a pure woman, for he depicts Phil as a young man out for a good time with the girls of Chicago. He hints at a past intimacy between Dolly and Phil—one which Phil fostered in spite of the fact that Dolly is the wife of one of his friends; but Kirkland removed a section of the original story which showed Dolly as the mother of a baby whose father might be Phil. Despite this omission Kirkland was actually more forthright about sex in *The McVeys* than in *Zury*, for he has Dr. Stafford instruct Phil about sex, and he later has the doctor discuss Phil's philandering in Chicago. Too, he uses Phil's relation to Dolly as a means of creating the circumstances of Phil's death at the hands of B'God Hobbs.

Hobbs is twisted, evil, and dark. He is a mean stepfather, a vicious neighbor, and a man who will sacrifice everything for the revenge of a self-defined wrong. The tone of his character is strange, for he is one of the unhinged, unhappy characters whose destiny is to play the part of villain. He is destroyed by his experience as a pioneer; he blames the world for his flaw in character, his inability to get on, and for being what he is. He is the product of an environment which has destroyed him; and he is more naturalistic than realistic.

The contrast in the characters in *The McVeys* indicates that Kirkland tried to reach in two directions—toward the commonplace and the smiling aspects of life and toward the dark underside of life which he also knew from experience to be a part of human character.

In summary, Kirkland tried in *The McVeys* to carry forward his ideas of fiction as an art which conceals a social study of life. He reveals the social stages which he suggested in *Zury*, but essentially he created a weak novel which has not been of much interest to later critics. Usually dismissed as a sequel to *Zury*, it deserves little more attention. The fact of the matter is that Kirkland's *Zury* did hang like a cloud over his later work and that the author was never able to get away from the shadow. He had, indeed, started too late in life to find enough material to produce another novel on the level of his first one. But, though he was aware of his weaknesses, he would not give up trying until he had written a story of his war experience.

III   *The Civil War Story*

The McVeys depleted Kirkland's material about farm and village life. He strained to force environment and character into focus in the novel, and he lost his power to portray the stark realism which he wanted. Having finished his attempts at life in the Middle West, he turned to his war experiences.

Encouraged by the reception of *Zury*, Kirkland had first toyed with the idea of a war novel in which he wanted to use Phil as the central character; but, since he had caused Phil to die in *The McVeys*, he had to search for a new character. As early as June, 1887, he had mentioned the idea to Garland; by February, 1888, he had begun the story, outlining his intent in a letter to Garland: "Perry Fenton, merchant turned soldier will be the hero. Don't know how much Zúry can do, at his age—over sixty. Poor Phil is dead or he would be the hero!"[16] By June, 1888, he stated that he had sacrificed too much of his story in an attempt to make it popular and that the novel was "merely a pot-boiler."[17] He had also renamed the hero, calling him William Faregon.

Because he was not able to sell the novel outright, he lifted several chapters from it for sale as short stories to the magazine *America*.[18] However, in September, 1889, the *Detroit Free Press* announced a contest in which the first prize was $1,600; and Kirkland entered his manuscript. After waiting anxiously for the results to be announced, he was at last informed that his story had taken first place over the seventy-eight other entries. The novel was then published serially beginning June 14, 1890, in the *Detroit Free Press*. In 1891 the Dibble Publishing Company of Chicago bought the work for publication in book form; and the original illustrations used in the serial were included.

When the book was published, the *Dial* critic suggested at once that Kirkland was the "Tolstoi of the West";[19] *The Critic* opined that the work was similar to that of Tolstoi and de

Maupassant;[20] but the *Bookbuyer* noted that the story, despite its realism, did not do justice to the material.[21] Kirkland had not produced the first realistic war novel, for this trend had been started with John W. De Forest's *Miss Ravenel's Conversion from Secession to Loyalty* (1865; 1867).

Actually, Kirkland's appraisal of *The Captain* as a potboiler was the correct one; the book, though it contains, as the *Bookbuyer* critic recognized, some good realistic descriptions, was not a successful work of art. Kirkland slipped into faults of proportion which make the novel ungainly and, though not ugly, artificial in its contrived romance and effect. Perhaps part of the difficulty artistically was that Kirkland still felt too strongly about the war and had too many vivid memories for him to master his subject or treat it objectively.

Kirkland appropriately dedicated *The Captain of Company K* "To the surviving men of the firing line; who could see the enemy in front of them with the naked eye, while they would have needed a field glass to see the history makers behind them."[22] In it, he called up his memories of the war, the stories which he had heard, his sense of dialect, and his hatred of war itself.

Making William Faregon his central character, he endowed him with the characteristics of Perry Fenton of *The McVeys*. Faregon helps raise a regiment of volunteers in Chicago, enlists himself, is elected captain of Company K, and moves with his company into training camp at Cairo, Illinois. He has left his merchandising company, his sweetheart Sara Penrose, and his friends in Chicago; and he finds himself facing a war which had seemed more a matter of enthusiasm than fact. Shortly after his arrival at camp he leads an advance scouting party, and he experiences his first taste of war—and discovers that it is entirely different from what he had expected. He returns to camp to find that his superiors take credit for his accomplishments, and he feels oddly out of place.

He manages to get leave to go to Chicago, and there he finds that the merchants are using the war to increase their profits. Since his own business is falling off because he is not there to manage it, he places it in the hands of a friend, an old Scot named Thorborn, who is a friend of Sara Penrose and her family. The old man saves as much of the business as he can; but he finally sells it to keep it from going under completely; and Faregon is relieved of worry about losing all his money.

When Faregon returns to camp, he takes part in the attack on Fort Donelson, the attack on Shiloh, and the siege of Vicksburg. He makes friends with Lt. McClintlock, one of his officers; and he recognizes Dr. Stafford (from *The McVeys*), who has become an army surgeon. Sara Penrose and her sister Lydia come to visit, and Lydia falls in love with McClintlock. He, however, is soon lost in battle, and Lydia, accompanied by Zury and Anne Prouder, search the battlefield but do not find his body. Grief-stricken, they return to Chicago.

When Faregon loses a leg in battle, he is assigned to Camp Douglas for recuperation. He sees all his friends, and he learns that Sara Penrose has been left a fortune by his old friend, Thorborn. He leaves the army and, disillusioned with the business world, studies medicine. He and Sara are married and settle in Chicago. McClintlock turns up—he had been captured in battle—and he and Lydia are married. Thus Faregon and Sara, Lydia and McClintlock find romantic happiness—and the story ends with an essay about the expansion of Chicago after the Civil War.

IV Narration, Plot, Style, Summary

The story of *The Captain* moves forward through episodes—battles and incidents of war—in the same manner as the other novels. As in *The McVeys*, Kirkland strung them on a thin line of romance which adds little but sentimentality to the story. He also used all the earlier devices—dialect, tales, humor—to carry the thread of the story. But in his descriptions told from the point of view of Faregon he is most effective. Yet because Kirkland found that he could not manipulate whole armies easily, he resorted to stage directions to indicate movement and as a result the work sometimes takes on the air of melodrama. He causes each scene to be acted out, and the set is changed at once to continue the action. The result is not every effective, for the continual confusion of setting the stage makes the resulting action unconvincing.

Kirkland soundly condemns war: "Whenever it shall become the rule that the man who causes a war shall be its first victim, war will be at an end" (p. 85). He felt with General Scott that war flourished mostly by the "fury of the non-combatants," and he called attention to the men who create war in order to make money. He noted that war is a "business-is-business" proposition to those who deal in contracts but that it is quite another thing to the soldier who faces the enemy on the battlefield.

Will Faregon discovers quickly that war is not the romantic thing which he and many others imagined. He tires of camp life and seeks refuge in Cairo in the old St. Charles Hotel where he finds a bed with a mattress, a mirror for shaving, and privacy—a luxury which he had almost forgotten. After a short stay he returns to camp to lead his men into battle and to have his first taste of bullets:

> He walked on, but more slowly. He instinctively directed his steps behind trees that stood where his way led. Then a bullet passed him at his own level—"Whip". Then another lodged in a tree—"Hitt". Then something struck lightly on his kepi—it was only a twig that had been cut off by one of the high-flying balls, but, at the same instant, "Spatt!" a bullet struck the ground at his right, and he pushed up to a tree in front of him and leaned, panting, against it, with both hands on the trunk. It was a white oak, and the rough gray bark impressed on his staring eyeballs a picture of its long, pointed, diamond-shaped corrugations, which he never forgot (p. 97).

Faregon nearly lost his nerve, and "he brought back his hand against the tree trunk; and between his thumbs pressed his forehead hard against the flinty bark, and rolled it from side to side, as if to get a little bodily pain to assuage his mental agony" (p. 97). Later, when his men think he has been wounded in battle, he is different from Henry Fleming in Stephen Crane's *The Red Badge of Courage*: Henry Fleming allows his comrades to believe the lie, but William Faregon reveals the source of the wounds on his forehead and tells how he got them.

Yet Faregon's scars are also red badges of courage, and later, when he loses his leg, he has another such badge.

Kirkland makes him, therefore, into a typical hero; but he is one who hates war and says so. Kirkland uses the other characters to voice the idea that war is confusion, error, and fright. The cowardice of the typical loudmouth, Calib Dugong, and the horror of the encounters with the dead and the wounded are presented in understatements which anticipate Stephen Crane; but Kirkland's artistry never approaches Crane's impressionism and control.

Some of the pictures recall the writing of John W. De Forest, especially the pictures of the wounded. For example, the description of a young man who is dying recalls the realism of De Forest: "A bullet had torn clean through his lungs, and the breath made a dreadful noise escaping through the wound at every exhalation" (p. 104). Fear dictates the feelings of the men, and in the midst of a shelling, Faregon "felt as if he could not hug mother earth closely enough—he would have liked to dig a hole, with his nails, to hide in" (p. 117).

But the thin romantic plot laid over the realism of the scenes of the battlefields spoils the novel; Kirkland could not resist trying to please the public. Furthermore, his vein of material having run thin, Kirkland edges Zury Prouder, Ann, and Dr. Stafford into *The Captain* in an attempt to endow it with the reality of his earlier novels. Because he uses too many incidents in the attempt to present action, the novel is never controlled and its impact is therefore diminished.

Despite these weaknesses, Kirkland does succeed in presenting a picture of war: the terrible waste of human life, the wanton destruction of property, and the feeling of nightmare of the common soldier. *The Captain of Company K*— despite its artistic crudities and a consequent lack of force —does create for the reader a sense of having been there. Neglected by most critics and historians except to be mentioned as part of Kirkland's work, *The Captain of Company K* could be considered as a possible analogue for Crane's more famous novel.[23]

With *The Captain of Company K*, Kirkland closed his career as a writer of fiction. His increasing interest in the factual had led him into citation of it and to photographic development of it; it was not odd, therefore, that he turned from writing fiction to recording history.

CHAPTER 7

The Final Years

BY 1889, when Kirkland wrote that his life had begun to take shape in a way which in previous years he would have been glad to foresee, he had become financially independent. The estate of his father-in-law, John Wilkinson, was settled that year; and Kirkland and his wife were recipients of about $200,000.[1] Furthermore, his law practice was increasingly lucrative because he had established a sound reputation in Chicago as a tax lawyer. He was in a position to turn his attention to things of special interest to him.

In 1889, having accepted the position of literary editor with the *Chicago Tribune,* he received the first words of commendation the paper had given to him; for on October 6, 1889, the *Tribune* published a pencil portrait of Kirkland and termed him the "Tolstoi of the West." As an editor of the paper he may have written special articles, but none of his work is signed. However, his connection with the paper led to his work as a special correspondent with the Warner Miller expedition to Central America.

Returning from that trip late in May, 1891, he found his brother William dying. William, knowing Joseph's financial circumstances, left his estate of $30,000 to the two Kirkland sisters, Elizabeth and Cordelia. In the same year, 1891, Louise, Kirkland's second daughter, married Victor C. Sanborn, of Lake Forest, Illinois, a lawyer whom she had met through her father. Caroline, the eldest daughter, who tried her hand at writing, became the famous "Madame X," the reporter of social events for the *Tribune.* Ethel, the youngest daughter, did not marry until ten years after Kirkland's death at which time, in 1904, she married a Briton and went to South Africa to live. John Kirkland, the son, trained in business by his father and in engineering at Cornell University, went at the turn of the century to South Africa with the General Electric Company.

In 1891 Joseph Kirkland was singularly free from worry for the first time in his life. And his interest in portraying life as faithfully as it was possible for him to reconstruct it led him quite naturally into the field of historical writing; for—as was noted earlier—he had long been interested in the history of Illinois and Chicago. Further stimulated to write the story of Chicago because the city planned to hold the Columbian Exposition and because he thought a good history of the city might sell well, he began in 1891 a two-volume history of the city.

I   *The Story of Chicago*

Kirkland decided to call his work *The Story of Chicago,* and he arranged with the Dibble Publishing Company, publishers of his last novel, to print the book, which appeared late in 1891. When the edition was exhausted, he re-edited the work in one volume in 1892.

His aim as a historian was clearly set forth in the preface to the first edition. He intended to be as accurate as possible, and he wrote:

> The best a historian can do is to approach accuracy before venturing upon publication; and, after publication, to approach it more and more nearly; for to reach it is beyond his utmost scope.
>
> The degree in which he can do this latter is dependent on the trouble his readers may take in pointing out his errors of omission and commission. "A word to the wise is sufficient"; and these words are addressed to all who are interested enough to read, wise enough to criticize and friendly enough to correct, for posterity, this "Story of Chicago."

The recital of Chicago's history began with a recounting of the geological formations surrounding the area of the city. Kirkland dwelt at length on the rivers and harbors and the part played by railroads which had spread in every direction from the city. He devoted a chapter to the Indian tribes, and then wrote of the explorations and settlements made by the French. Retelling the part played by the Illinois country in the Revolutionary War, he detailed the events which brought about the massacre at old Fort Dearborn, noting in Chapter VIII all the material which he later used for a publication on the subject. He added personal touches, for he recalled his own experiences and included letters written by members of his own family as well as newspaper accounts and oral traditions which threw light on the past life of the city.

Having long been interested in the Chicago Historical Society which had been founded in 1856, Kirkland found much in its collection to interest him. The fire of 1871 had destroyed all the records of the society, including the famous first draft of Lincoln's Emancipation Proclamation; but after 1871 the library of the society was started anew. In July, 1874, a fire destroyed the library once more. Kirkland helped to found a third library for the society, contributing as much as he could from his own funds and collecting money and materials from others. He remembered that an old friend of his father had often expressed interest in historical matters, and he wrote to him, asking that funds for a library building be donated if possible. That man, Henry D. Gilpin, a former solicitor of the treasury of the United States, responded by giving a considerable amount of money to the society to use in restoring the library. Others added to the fund, and by the middle of the 1870's it amounted to $72,000.[2] Much of the material which Kirkland helped to collect for the library later aided him in his writing of history.

One source which Kirkland used was a file of pamphlets published over a period of time beginning in the 1850's by John Fergus, a printer who had settled at an early date in Chicago. Fergus, believing that many persons were interested in the earlier days of the city, published legends of the Indians, the story of French settlements in the locality, and accounts of the Massacre of 1812 in a series which he called the *Fergus Historical Series*.[3]

Kirkland gleaned further information from old settlers, especially such men as Judge Dean Caton, a former justice of the Supreme Court of Illinois, who was still in Chicago. Judge Caton had first come to the city in 1833, when the Indian tribes—the Potawatomies and the Ottawas—were still in the vicinity, and Kirkland spent many hours listening to his stories of his early days. Kirkland supplemented his subject matter obtained from such persons with material from Theodore Roosevelt's *The Winning of the West*[4] and, as we shall see, from his own memories.

For Kirkland himself had been in the vicinity of Chicago since 1856, and he could tell of the city as he remembered it. His memories of the past gave color and reality to his record. Remembering the panics which had gripped the city in the early days, he illustrated his points with anecdotes which he had heard during the time he worked as an auditor for the Illinois Central Railroad. He recalled Fort Dearborn, the Civil War days of the city, the first steam railroads which came into the city, the steam engine *Pioneer*, and the entertainment, fires, social clubs, parks, riots, and strikes which he had observed. He recalled some of the great men of the past and his experiences with them, especially William B. Ogden, who had founded the Northwestern Railroad and whose great house, which now houses the Newberry Library, was the meeting place for politicians and businessmen of the nation.[6]

He noted the social organizations, and he once more expressed his dislike for labor organizations, retelling in detail the story of the Haymarket riot of May 4, 1886, as he remembered it.[7] He wrote that for some time there had been unrest among the laboring men of the city for, as May Day—designated by the Federation of Trades for the inauguration of a strike for an eight-hour day—approached, tension grew all over the city. Police squads were increased after April 26, when working men marched in a procession to the lake front where eight thousand persons assembled to listen to labor leaders. May Day passed without trouble, but on May 3 pickets at the McCormick plant were shot at by the police and several men were killed.

As a result, a great mass meeting was held by the workers the following evening, May 4, to "denounce the latest acts of the police"—according to August V. T. Spies, editor of the

Arbeiter Zeitung—and the use of force was urged as a cure for the situation which so dissatisfied the workmen. Carter Harrison, mayor of Chicago, took measures to keep the meeting peaceful by instructing the police to take no actions to interfere with the crowd. But Bonfield, an inspector in the police department, marshalled one hundred and twenty-five policemen and marched on the meeting to disperse it. In the resulting confusion a bomb was thrown among the police, killing one man outright and fatally injuring others. At once the police began to arrest men whom they considered responsible. August Spies, Albert Parsons, Samuel Fielden, and four others, Engel, Fischer, Lingg, and Schwab—all members of the Black International, an anarchist organization with headquarters in Chicago—were arrested and held for trial.

Beginning on June 7, their trial lasted sixty-two days. The state used one hundred and forty-three witnesses; the defense, seventy-nine. No proof could be found that any one of the accused was involved in the bomb-throwing episode. Julius S. Grinnell acted as the State's Attorney, and Judge Joseph E. Gary was the presiding judge. Swayed by the public reaction to the anarchists, Judge Gary found the men guilty under a new and peculiar interpretation of the law which declared that the men were guilty if they had incited others to violence. Five of the men were sentenced to hang. On of them, Louis Lingg, committed suicide in his cell. Four others, Parsons, Spies Engel, and Fischer, were hanged; but Fielden and Schwab had their sentences commuted to life imprisonment.

Judge Gary's interpretation of the law brought an outcry from liberals all over the country, but Joseph Kirkland was not one of them. In 1891, in his history, he declared that "the wise, able and correct rulings, of the veteran Judge Joseph E. Gary were the efficient cause of making the proceedings invulnerable on the review of the Supreme Court," and that because of the "exhaustive analysis" of Judge Gary's court, in the future the "world will probably come to the conclusion that justice was done."[8]

Kirkland thought that the trial was not very important; the most noteworthy thing to him was

. . . not the conduct of the offenders, or of the police, but of the true working masses of the City, State, and Country, not one of whom raised hand or voice to defend these "Saviors of Labor," or made any public utterance except to disclaim part or lot in the effort to disturb the law of the land; that system of government wherein they and each of them has his share of control through the ballot box.[9]

Kirkland must have known of and deliberately ignored the protest which came from William Dean Howells, who publicly denounced the "principle" of hanging men because of "their frantic opinions, for a crime which they were not shown to have committed." At any rate, Kirkland was mistaken about the attitude of future generations, to say nothing of his own contemporaries; for two years later in 1893 Governor John P. Altgeld pardoned the men who were serving prison sentences for having incited others to violence in connection with the riot.

When Kirkland related the particulars of the work of George Pullman and his factory system, he concluded that the town of Pullman was the best place in which a laborer could live because it was carefully controlled. He ignored the dreadful conditions of the housing and praised the scheme as the beginning of "cooperation between labor and capital."[10] If he ignored the fact that Pullman ruled like a divine-right king in the town and instituted a system of spying among his laborers, it was because Kirkland thought it was the right of an employer to do as he wished.

Kirkland, as might be expected, also declared that American workingmen were not really interested in labor unions, which were a "foreign idea" brought in by "walking outsiders" who were trying to destroy the "American Idea" of free enterprise and freedom to work. Although Kirkland aligned himself with employers against the rising tide of labor unions, his attitude was not a new one in his family; his mother had made herself unpopular by insisting that the laborer was morally obliged to do the work given him by his employer. And Kirkland followed her in citing the growth of the city as an illustration of "how hard men work when they are free to work, and how strong and supple their muscles and minds grow by use in their self-imposed tasks."[11]

The Story of Chicago was sent by Mr. Dibble to many persons in the East for criticism.[12] Oliver Wendell Holmes wrote that "it is indeed a story worth telling, and I thank you most heartily for giving me the opportunity of placing it upon my shelves." Louise Chandler Moulton said that "it interested me more than any other story of a town that I have ever read," and she congratulated the publisher on having secured "so accomplished a writer as Major Kirkland, whose novels are a memorable delight," and "who proves himself, in this fascinating 'Story of Chicago' no less successful as a historian." Frances Willard, writing from Rest Cottage, Evanston, Illinois, thought that "whoever helps to put this book under eyes that have not been blessed by its fair, inspiring pages and choice photogravures has helped to increase the sum of human happiness."

E. C. Stedman told the publisher that "when you prevailed upon Major Kirkland to write the 'Story of Chicago' you displayed once more your acumen. You induced the brilliant author of 'Zury' to forgo his imaginative work for a while, and to devote his talent to the narration of an 'o'er true tale'—a tale, however, as strange and as absorbing as any romance. I know he will get his reward, and I hope you will get yours." Stedman continued to praise the work as an example of "liberality and taste" in its illustrations. "Every American is proud of Chicago, of her history, her great ambition, her financial and intellectual progress. Her record is faithfully set forth in your handsome volume. Whoever designs to visit Chicago . . . should own and thoroughly read 'The Story'."

II *The Massacre of 1812*

The success of his first history greatly pleased Kirkland, and he began to investigate source material about the Chicago Massacre of 1812, the histories of which had not satisfied him while he was writing his history of the city. He found a record of the massacre in pamphlet Number 16 of the *Fergus Historical Series* by John Wentworth; he hunted up a novel, *Wau-Bun*, published in 1854 by Mrs. John H. Kinzie, in which its story was told; but he deemed these works inaccurate. When he learned that Darius Heald, the son of

Captain Nathan Heald, was living in Missouri, he brought him to Chicago to tell the story as he had heard it from his father who was in the fight. Kirkland wrote about his information from Heald: "his repetition of that story, taken down in shorthand from his own lips, forms the main part of the strictly new matter I offer in this book."[13] But he also secured the muster roll of Fort Dearborn from the War Department archives, and he included a complete transcript of it in an appendix.

As a result of his researches, Kirkland concluded that "history is not a snapshot. Events happen, and the true record of them follows at a distance." He then described further his idea of the task of the historian: "Sometimes the early report is too voluminous, and it takes time to reduce it to truth by a winnowing process that divides chaff from grain. This has been the case regarding every great modern battle. Sometimes, on the other hand, the event was obscure and became important through the rise of other later conditions; in which case, instead of winnowing, the historian sets himself to gleaning the field and making his grist out of scattered bits of its fruitage. This has been the case regarding the Chicago massacre of 1812. . . ."[14]

As a result of his "gleaning" Kirkland retold Wentworth's version of the massacre in fifty pages and followed it with the story he had taken down from the younger Heald. Retelling the story of the battle, he followed each principal white participant to his or her fate. In the second part of the work he presented historical and narrative events pertinent to the massacre, and he reported the building and abandonment of Fort Dearborn. From the *Buffalo Gazette* of April 13, 1813, and of June 4, 1814, he reprinted the story as that paper had copied it from the October 12, 1812, issue of *Niles' Weekly Register*. Among the sketches of early settlers of Chicago, he included one of Mrs. John Kinzie as it had appeared in the *Fergus Historical Series*, Number 10. He included not only the report of the officials of the Indian Commission but the photographs of each of the principal persons killed in the massacre.

In the appendices he printed brief sketches of the families: the Whistlers, Kinzies, Wellses, and Healds. He included an account of a grave discovered near Cass and Illinois streets in Chicago. Kirkland had rescued the bones from the hands of workingmen who had found the grave; had sought to identify them as those of John Lalime, a government employe who had served as an interpreter at Fort Dearborn; and had given the bones to the Chicago Historical Society for future use. He also recalled that models for the bronze statue which marks the spot where Fort Dearborn once stood were two Indians, Kicking Bear and Short Bull, who had been captured in a disturbance at Pine Ridge and Wounded Knee Creek; and he identified the figure of the man at the feet of the woman (Mrs. Helm) as Surgeon Van Voorhees, the doctor of the garrison at the time of the massacre. The appendices covered nearly as many pages as the actual history, but they helped round out the factual material which Kirkland wanted to make available to his readers. The result of his work is a clear, readable history of the massacre.

III *The Last Project*

After *The Massacre of 1812* Kirkland turned to larger projects. In connection with his work with the Chicago Historical Society, he had come to know John Moses, the librarian, who had been an official historian of the state of Illinois and who had published a two-volume work, *Illinois, Historical and Statistical* (1889). Moses suggested to Kirkland that an official history of Chicago be undertaken, and Kirkland, eager to continue his writing of history, consented to become a co-editor of a work which would bring together a group of essays, newspaper reports, and other material. He began the writing of the five opening chapters of the work which was to be called *History of Chicago* and which Munsell's Publishing Company agreed to publish.

But in the midst of his work for this history, Kirkland became ill. For some time he had been bothered with abscessed teeth, and at last he decided to have them extracted. He appeared to recover from the operation, and after a few days he was able to go out to a barber shop to have his beard trimmed. By the evening of April 27 he was apparently in good health, for he was able to take part in a family dinner and in the conversation which followed. But about five o'clock the following morning, April 28, 1894, he suffered a severe heart attack and died almost at once.[15] The funeral was held at the family residence, 161 Rush Street, at two o'clock on Tuesday, May 1, 1894. The Reverend David Swing, a friend of long standing, officiated; and the pallbearers were Judge Mark Bangs, August W. Eddy, Charles B. King, J. L. Silshes, J. C. Shortall, Henry W. King, Colonel Huntington, W. Jackson, and H. D. Hosmer. He was buried in Graceland Cemetery.

Kirkland's autobiographical sketch, in preparation for inclusion in the *History of Chicago*, lay unfinished on his desk. Caroline, his daughter, not only finished the work but took her father's place as co-editor of the history.

IV *The Path Marked Out—an Estimate*

Although Joseph Kirkland had not finished his history, he had already carved his place in the historical development of literature of the Middle West. Before long he was overshadowed by more productive writers, and scholarly attention has been directed to him only with the realization that a nation produces a mature literature slowly, that a new national literature is apt to be different from other national literatures, and that essentially the quality of American literature in its full bloom of maturity is composed of a quest for reality which is the intrinsic value apparent in the life and work of Joseph Kirkland.

Kirkland's three novels were his most important literary activity. He made his environment an essential part of his fiction, and he standardized dialect in his work. He rose above mere local color, for his characters were alive, real flesh and blood, and faced with problems of a typical nature. He followed the path marked out by his mother in drawing his characters, his dialect, and his scenes from reality; but he became a leader in the writing of realistic fiction in the Middle West, and he found a place as the first professional writer of Chicago.

Faithful to the instinct for telling the truth and plagued by the chasm between artist and the capitalist society which was characteristic of the age, Kirkland did not shrink from doing what he felt to be a moral duty: he wrote in protest against the hardness and meanness of life. He himself was touched and wasted by some necessity to earn a living; he was also under the compulsion to become "someone"; to carry on his slightly snobbish family insistence about being urbane, however vaguely; and to mix and mingle with the society of Chicago as his family had done in Philadelphia and New York.

Forced as a young man to begin to earn his own uncertain fortune in the world, he experienced bitter frustration in his career. In the end his stubbornness and his insistence on trying had brought him through so that at the age of fifty he no longer had to take hand-me-down cases of Mark Bangs; and he could, indeed, turn his attention to the formation of literary clubs; practice at playwrighting; and hope, however vainly, that he could turn out novels of truly great worth. But the stark, almost unbearably dull life, the straight white road of exhausting work, the wringing of wealth from the black, root-tangled soil of Illinois gave him the sense of starved life which he needed to write his novels. Too, his careful adoption of a medium in dialect, the constant practice of it, the careful standardizing of it in order to give his characters verisimilitude, helped him bring them into being as living creatures in his somewhat turgid work. And they endow the novels with true realistic pictures of life as it was.

What the exact intent of the novelist is—what the aim of the novel as an art form is—may not have been answered by Kirkland's work. But that he contributed to the larger pattern—that he gave his small contribution to the whole figure in the carpet—is certain. The aim of his work was to portray society, to present character as it partook of society, to build through incident and tall tale and humor the very life of his characters and the quality of his societies. That he succeeded is apparent to the reader of his novels today—especially to the reader of *Zury*. For though all his work has the imprint of its era and of the limitations of its author, it bears equally the stamp of authenticity and of the struggle of the artist to create. For though Kirkland's pictures are for the most part —as he himself thought—not dramatic, they create the sense for the reader of having been there and of having lived through things as they were. The naive society of his work is the forerunner of the society of today, and only a few of our present-day novelists have been able to emotionalize much better than Kirkland. No writer has been more honest though the results are sometimes primitive in their crudeness.

Certainly there can be little doubt that Kirkland is important, first, as a novelist who set down life in the Middle West in early days. Secondly, he is important because he influenced Hamlin Garland to turn to the writing of fiction in order to depict actual farm life. Thirdly, he is important because he made use of dialect and of particular settings to bring to his readers the problems of life which men and women in rude surroundings everywhere must face and solve. Moreover he tried to standardize the dialect in order to reflect the harsh constriction of pioneer life and to suggest the waste of finer values exacted by the prairies.

He used the prairies for his setting because he knew them thoroughly from his own observation. He recorded customs and lives of pioneers of Illinois, the dreadful hardships of poverty, and the fight for survival by men and women confronted by a raw environment. He made his people subject to the influences of circumstance and accident; but he portrayed them as capable of rising above the deterministic and sordid narrowness of such influences. He used the primitive and elemental forces of nature to create the real; and, though his weak men fall in their battle with the elemental, those of strength and courage win the fight to control their own destinies.

Kirkland selected the episodes in his stories to make a plea for charity, for understanding, and for the repudiation of narrow traditional practices which turn both truth and reality into falsehood and hypocrisy for the sake of appearance. He pleaded for the sympathetic human heart: for the hand of brotherhood freely extended to suffering men and women everywhere. He made Zury Prouder, his greatest character, into a man who, having turned a naturally generous nature into the narrow channels which molds him into a skinflint moneygrubber, finds the qualities of generosity restored to him through love.

Kirkland was not a great writer, for he began to write

too late in life to acquire mastery of his medium. Yet he pictured life in all its essential struggles: his Zury and his Anne are a real man and a real woman who rise from the surroundings in which they are submerged—and with a struggle which itself gives dignity to their lives. Out of experience and hardships, out of the division of forces within man himself, out of disappointments and sufferings, Joseph Kirkland revealed that man becomes noble when he battles to conquer himself and the world around him in a search for spiritual freedom in the realm of immaterial reality.

Notes and References

Chapter One

1. Hamlin Garland, *Roadside Meetings* (New York, 1931), p. 111.

2. Hobart Chatfield-Taylor to Winifred Wilson, Wilson Collection.

3. Garland, *op. cit.*, p. 111.

4. See V. C. Sanborn, "The Kirtland or Kirkland Family," reprinted from the *New England Historical and Genealogical Register* (January, 1894); *The Dictionary of American Biography*, X, 432; Clayton A. Holaday, "Joseph Kirkland: Biography and Criticism," (unpublished Ph.D. dissertation, Department of English, University of Indiana, 1949).

5. Caroline M. Kirkland, *A New Home—Who'll Follow?* (5th ed.; New York, 1855), p. 50. See also her *Western Clearings* (New York, 1846), pp. 2-14.

6. *A New Home*, p. 47.

7. *Ibid.*, p. 67.

8. *Land Records*, Livingstone County Records, Michigan Historical Records.

9. Autobiographical sketch in the Kirkland Papers in the Newberry Library, Chicago, Illinois. Henceforth these papers will be referred to simply as the Kirkland Papers.

10. *A New Home*, Preface.

11. Kirkland Papers.

12. Kirkland Papers.

13. Journal fragment, Kirkland Papers.

14. *Putnam's Monthly Magazine*, I (January, 1853), 2.

15. Frank Luther Mott, *A History of American Magazines* (Cambridge, Mass., 1938), II, 423.

16. Kirkland Papers.

17. Joseph Kirkland, *The Captain of Company K* (Chicago, 1891), p. 12.

18. *Ibid.*, p. 32.

19. *Adjutant General's Report, Illinois* (Springfield, 1867), I, 205, 315. See also, George B. McClellan, *McClellan's Own Story* (New York, 1887), p. 122.

20. *The Prairie Chicken*, I, No. 10 (July, 1865).

21. *Ibid.*

22. United States Congress, *Senate Document,* No. 37, Parts 1-2, 46th Congress, 1st Session (Washington, 1879), p. 446. See also, *War of Rebellion, Official Records,* (published under the direction of the Secretary of War; Washington: Government Printing Office, 1880-1881), Series I, XI, Part 11, 226.

Chapter Two

1. Statement by Louise Kirkland Sanborn in a personal interview with Winifred Wilson; in the possession of Miss Wilson.

2. Joseph Kirkland to the Adjutant General, February 22, 1863, in the Department of Records, Office of the Adjutant General, Department of Army, Washington, D. C.

3. Oscar Fay Adams, "Caroline Matilda Kirkland," *The Christian Register,* April 16, 1914, p. 370.

4. Autobiographical sketch, Kirkland Papers.

5. *The Prairie Chicken,* I, No. 1 (October 1, 1864). See also, Thomas O. Mabbott and Philip D. Jordan, *"The Prairie Chicken," Journal of the Illinois State Historical Society,* XXV, No. 3 (October, 1932), 155.

6. *The Prairie Chicken,* I, No. 3 (December 1, 1864).

7. Mabbott and Jordan, *op. cit.,* p. 155.

8. *The Prairie Chicken,* I, No. 1 (October 1, 1864).

9. Mabbott and Jordon, *op. cit.,* point out that the paper was once thought to be lost completely, for Scott, in *Newspapers and Periodicals of Illinois, Illinois Historical Collections,* VI, *Biographical Series,* I (Springfield: 1910) 316b, said that he could find no file of it. Daniel C. Haskell (compiler), *Checklist of Newspapers and Official Gazettes in the New York Public Library* (New York, 1915), p. 166, indicated its existence in that library; Mabbott and Jordan found the file which Haskell noted. I have used one unknown to them which is in the Chicago Public Library in which the notations in the margins are in the hand of Cordelia Kirkland.

10. *The Prairie Chicken,* I, No. 1 (October 1, 1864).

11. *Ibid.,* I, No. 2 (November 1, 1864).

12. *Ibid.*

13. *Ibid.,* I, No. 8 (May 1, 1865).

14. *Ibid.,* I, No. 9 (June 1, 1865).

15. *Ibid.,* I, No. 8 (May 1, 1865).

16. *Ibid.,* I, No. 4 (January 1, 1865).

17. Joseph Kirkland, *Zury: The Meanest Man in Spring County, A Novel of Western Life* (Boston, 1887), pp. 55-56.

18. *The Prairie Chicken,* I, No. 9 (June 1, 1865).

19. *Ibid.*, I, No. 12 (September, 1865).

20. See Mabbott and Jordan, *op. cit.*, 164-66.

21. *The Prairie Chicken, I*, No. 9 (June 1, 1865); No. 10 (July 1, 1865); No. 11 (August 1, 1865).

22. Ernest L. Bogart and Charles Manfred Thompson, *The Industrial State, The Centennial History of Illinois* (Springfield, 1920), IV, 401.

23. *Ibid.*, p. 315.

24. *Ibid.*, p. 363.

25. Vermilion County, Illinois, *Register of Deeds*, VIII, 356.

26. Hiram W. Beckwith, *History of Vermilion County, Illinois* (Chicago, 1879), 426-27.

27. Vermilion County, Illinois, *Register of Deeds*, VIII, 347, 356; XII, 279.

28. See Russel B. Nye, *George Bancroft, Brahmin Rebel* (New York, 1945), pp. 241-79.

29. Joseph Kirkland, *The Story of Chicago* (2nd ed.; Chicago: Dibble Publishing Company, 1892), p. 251.

30. Bogart and Thompson, *op. cit.*, pp. 29-31; see also, Ealias Colbert and Everett Chamberlin, *Chicago and the Great Conflagration* (Cincinnati, 1872), for a detailed history of the fire.

31. Letter of Cordelia Kirkland to cousins in Utica, New York, quoted in Joseph Kirkland, *The Story of Chicago*, pp. 296-97.

32. Kirkland, *The Story of Chicago*, p. 304 n.

33. *Ibid.*, pp. 304-5 n.

34. Colbert and Chamberlin, *op. cit.*, p. 306, point out that only one coal yard, that of Botsford, Kimball & Company, was insured.

35. *Ibid.*, pp. 304-23.

36. Bogart and Thompson, *op. cit.*, pp. 84-86.

37. *Chicago Tribune*, January 1, 1876.

38. Kirkland, *The Story of Chicago*, p. 167.

39. *Ibid.*, p. 286.

40. Records of the Illinois Circuit Court, Danville, Illinois, Box 28, Document 1; Box 32, Documents 1-5. In Box 28 some of the documents are missinng.

41. A. T. Andreas, *History of Chicago* (3 vols.; Chicago, 1886), III, 565.

42. See, Ellis Paxson Oberholtzer, *A History of the United States Since the Civil War* (5 vols.; New York, 1926), III, 144 ff.

43. Andreas, *op. cit.*, III, 565.

44. Clipping in the Kirkland Papers, dated but not identified as to source; see also, Vermilion County, Illinois, *Register of Deeds*, XLIX, 398.

45. *Ibid.*

46. John Moses and Joseph Kirkland (eds.), *History of Chicago* (2 vols.; Chicago, 1895), I, 530. See also, *Chicago Tribune,* September 14, 1877.

47. *Chicago Tribune,* November 5, 1877; November 7, 1877; November 10, 1877.

48. Autobiographical sketch, Kirkland Papers.

49. *Ibid.*

Chapter Three

1. Moses and Kirkland (eds.), *op. cit.,* II, 582; see also the *Chicago Tribune,* January 2, 14, 16, 18, 1875; September 1, 1875.

2. *Chicago Tribune,* January 12, 1875; September 12, 1875; December 20, 1875.

3. *Chicago Tribune,* May 1, 1894.

4. David Swing, "Memorial to Joseph Kirkland," *Biographical Pamphlets: Chicago Literary Club,* read at a meeting of the club on Monday, May 28, 1894.

5. Joseph Kirkland, "An Experiment in Play Writing," *Atlantic Monthly,* XLIV, No. cclxii (August, 1879), 149-55.

6. *Ibid.,* p. 151.

7. *Chicago Tribune,* December 9, 1877.

8. *Ibid.,* December 11, 1877.

9. *Ibid.,* December 13, 1877.

10. *Ibid.,* December 14, 1877.

11. Kirkland, *Atlantic Monthly,* XLIV, 155; see above, note No. 5.

12. *Chicago Tribune,* January 22, 1919.

13. John T. Flinn, *Chicago, The Marvelous City of the West* (Chicago, 1892), p. 252.

14. *The Chicago Post,* February 26, 1893; *Contributors' Magazine,* I, No. 1 (February, 1893).

15. *Figaro,* March, 1893.

16. *Dial,* I (June, 1880), 30-33.

17. *Ibid.,* I (August, 1880), 67-69.

18. *Ibid.,* I (October, 1880), 110-12.

19. *Ibid.,* I (March, 1881), 233-36.

20. *Ibid.,* II (September, 1881), 93-94.

21. *Ibid.,* II (September, 1881), 57-59.

22. *Ibid.,* IV (December, 1883), 190-92.

23. *Ibid.,* VII (August, 1886), 79-81.

24. *Ibid.,* VII (April, 1887), 285-88.

25. *Ibid.,* VIII (October, 1887), 19-21.

26. *Ibid.,* VIII (April, 1888), 288-90.

27. *Ibid.*, X (October, 1889), 125-27.
28. *Ibid.*, XIV (May, 1893), 275-78.
29. *Figaro*, V (March, 1892), 168 ff.
30. *Figaro*, V (May, 1892), 168.
31. *McClure's Magazine*, September, 1893, pp. 555-60.
32. Copy in Kirkland Papers.
33. *Scribner's Magazine*, XII (July, 1892), 3-27.
34. *Critic*, November, 1893, p. 337.
35. *New England Magazine*, August, 1893, pp. 726-42.
36. *Century Magazine*, XXIV, No. 2 (June, 1883), 318-19.
37. *Contributors' Magazine*, May 16, 1894. Copy dated 1876 in the Kirkland Papers.
38. Unpublished MS, Kirkland Papers.
39. *America*, I (May, 1888), 6 ff.
40. *America*, I (December, 1888), 9 ff.
41. See Holaday, "Joseph Kirkland," pp. 191 ff.
42. *Western Clearings*, pp. 144-52.
43. Kirkland gives the information in a footnote in the novel.
44. *Chicago Tribune*, April 5, 8, 19, 24, 29; May 3, 10, 17, 31; June 7, 1891.

Chapter Four

1. The most useful studies on Howells and realism are Everett Carter, *Howells and the Rise of Realism* (New York, 1954); Edwin Cady, *The Road to Realism: The Early Years, 1837-1885, of William Dean Howells* (Syracuse, N. Y., 1957), and *The Realist at War: The Mature Years, 1885-1920, of William Dean Howells* (Syracuse, N. Y.; 1959); and Louis Wann, *The Rise of Realism* (2 vols.; New York, 1933).
2. *Dial*, XIV (February 16, 1893), 99-101.

Chapter Five

1. Letter to his wife, October 7, 1883, Kirkland Papers.
2. Letter to Louise C. Schuler, July 15, 1887, Kirkland Papers.
3. *The Critic*, X, No. 177 (May 21, 1887), 254; the reviewer used Kirkland's manuscript before the novel was revised for publication. In *Critic*, XI, No. 183 (July 22, 1887), the reviewer points to his error, made, he says, in the hope of saving time.
4. Reprinted as an advertisement in Kirkland, *The Chicago Massacre;* original in the *Boston Transcript*, May 16, 1887. I have kept the original spelling of the names of the Russian authors.
5. Hamlin Garland, *Roadside Meetings*, p. 106. See also

Garland, *A Son of the Middle Border* (New York, 1917), p. 354, for a slightly different version.

6. Letter to wife, June 22, 1887, Kirkland Papers.

7. Letter to daughter Ethel, June 29, 1887, Kirkland Papers.

8. Letter to his sister-in-law, Dorothy Wilkinson, June 29, 1887, Kirkland Papers.

9. Garland, *Roadside Meetings*, p. 106.

10. Joseph Kirkland to Hamlin Garland, May 31, 1887. The Kirkland letters to Hamlin Garland were made available to me by Professor Eldon C. Hill, Oxford, Ohio, who had the originals in his possession for some time before Garland's death. He furnished me with typescripts, copies of which are in the Kirkland Papers, Newberry Library, where I deposited them. The originals are in the Garland Papers, Doheny Library, The University of Southern California.

11. Garland, *Roadside Meetings*, p. 106.

12. *Ibid.*, pp. 106 ff.

13. Letter to wife, July, 1887, Kirkland Papers.

14. Letter to Garland, September 16, 1887.

15. Letter to Garland, November 13, 1887.

16. Letter to wife, July, 1887, Kirkland Papers.

17. See *Nation*, XLV (July 21, 1887), 37.

18. *Critic*, X, No. 177 (May 21, 1887), 254; XI, No. 183 (July 22, 1887).

19. *Dial*, VIII (July, 1887), 67.

20. *Overland Monthly*, X (August, 1887), 214-16.

21. *Harper's Monthly Magazine*, LXXVII (June, 1888), 153.

22. Joseph Kirkland, *Zury: The Meanest Man in Spring County, A Novel of Western Life* (rev. ed., Boston, 1887).

23. Letter to Garland, May 31, 1887.

24. *Chicago Daily News*, October 26, 1926.

25. Benjamin Lease, "Realism and Joseph Kirkland's *Zury*," *American Literature*, XXIII, No. 4 (January, 1952), 464-66; for treatment of the novel as a transition novel, see, Kenneth J. La Budde, "A Note on the Text of Joseph Kirkland's *Zury*," *American Literature*, XX (January, 1949), 452; and Henry Nash Smith, "The Western Farmer in Imaginative Literature, 1818-1891," *Mississippi Valley Historical Review*, XXXVI (December, 1949), 487.

26. Carter, *op. cit.*, has an excellent study of literary convention of the times.

27. Vernon Louis Parrington, *Main Currents in American Literature* (3 vols.; New York, 1927-1930), III, 391.

28. Joseph Kirkland, *Zury: The Meanest Man in Spring County*,

A Novel of Western Life. Facsimile Reprint with an Introduction by John T. Flanagan (Urbana, Ill., 1956), xvii.

29. Lloyd Lewis, "Letters of A Pioneer Realist," *The Newberry Library Bulletin,* No. 3 (December, 1945), pp. 3-7.

30. Dorothy A. Dondore, *The Prairie and the Making of Middle America* (Cedar Rapids, Iowa, 1926), pp. 325-26.

31. Lucy Lockwood, *The Frontier in American Literature* (New York, 1927), p. 262.

32. Arthur Hobson Quinn, *American Fiction: An Historical and Critical Survey* (New York, 1936), pp. 453-54.

33. Carl Van Doren, *The American Novel* (rev. ed.; New York, 1933), p. 196.

34. Alexander Cowie, *The American Novel,* "American Literature Series"; general editor, Harry H. Clark (New York, 1948), pp. 226-27.

35. *Literary History of the United States,* eds. Robert E. Spiller, Willard Thorp, Thomas H. Johnson, and Henry Seidel Canby (3 vols.; New York, 1948), II, 794; III, 319.

36. Henry Nash Smith, *Virgin Land, The American West As Myth and Symbol* (Cambridge, Mass., 1950), pp. 283-85.

37. Alfred Kazin, *On Native Grounds, An Interpretation of Modern American Prose Literature* (New York, 1956), pp. 13-14.

38. Bernard Duffy, *The Chicago Renaissance in American Letters, A Critical History* (East Lansing, Mich., 1954), pp. 93-98.

Chapter Six

1. Letter to daughter Caroline, June 17, 1887, Kirkland Papers.

2. Letter to family, June 20, 1887, Kirkland Papers.

3. Letter to family, June 22, 1887, Kirkland Papers.

4. Letter to sister-in-law, Dorothy Wilkinson, July 2, 1887, Kirkland Papers.

5. Letter to Louise Schuler, July 15, 1887, Kirkland Papers.

6. Letter to Garland, February 13, 1888.

7. Letter to Garland, March 5, 1888.

8. Letter to Garland, March 20, 1888.

9. Letter to Garland, March 28, 1888.

10. Joseph Kirkland, *The McVeys: An Episode* (Boston, 1888), p. 1.

11. Letter to wife, September 30, 1888, Kirkland Papers.

12. *Harper's Monthly Magazine,* LXXVII (May, 1889), 986.

13. *Dial,* IX (November, 1889), 161.

14. *Atlantic Monthly,* LXIII (February, 1889), 276-80.

15. *Overland Monthly*, XIII (January, 1888), 213-14.
16. Letter to Garland, March 28, 1888.
17. Letter to Garland, June 9, 1888.
18. See, Clayton A. Holaday, "Kirkland's *Captain of Company K*: A Twice-Told Tale," *American Literature*, XX (1956), 62-66; Clayton A. Holaday, "Joseph Kirkland's Company K," *Journal of the Illinois State Historical Society*, XLIX (1956), 256-307.
19. Cited in *Detroit Free Press*, September 22, 1889.
20. *Critic*, November 14, 1891.
21. *Bookbuyer*, November, 1891, p. 425.
22. Joseph Kirkland, *The Captain of Company K* (Chicago, 1891), p. 97.
23. Eric Soloman, "Another Analogue for *The Red Badge of Courage*," *Nineteenth Century Fiction*, XIII (1958), 63-66.

Chapter Seven

1. Dudley Wilkinson, Mrs. Kirkland's brother, had used funds from the estate before the will was probated; the result was that technical difficulties prevented the settlement for some years.
2. Joseph Kirkland, *The Story of Chicago* (2nd ed.; Chicago, 1891), pp. 343-44.
3. A file of the series is in the Chicago Historical Society Library.
4. Kirkland, *The Story of Chicago*, p. 37.
5. *Ibid.*, p. 37, as an example.
6. *Ibid.*, p. 145.
7. *Ibid.*, Chapter XXXII.
8. *Ibid.*, pp. 376-77.
9. *Ibid.*, pp. 387-88.
10. *Ibid.*, pp. 396-97.
11. *Ibid.*, pp. 440-41.
12. The letters to Mr. Dibble are printed in Joseph Kirkland, *The Chicago Massacre of 1812* (Chicago, 1893), p. 220.
13. Kirkland, *The Chicago Massacre of 1812*, p. 6.
14. *Ibid.*, p. 5.
15. *The Chicago Tribune*, April 30, 1894.

Selected Bibliography

PRIMARY SOURCES

Books

Zury: The Meanest Man in Spring County. Boston and New York: Houghton, Mifflin and Company, 1887. Revised ed., 1887; reprinted in 1889, 1892.

The McVeys: An Episode. Boston and New York: Houghton Mifflin and Company, 1888.

The Story of Chicago. Chicago: The Dibble Publishing Company, 1891. 2 vols. Revised ed. (1 vol.), 1892.

The Captain of Company K. Chicago: The Dibble Publishing Company, 1891. Published serially in *The Detroit Free Press*, June 14-July 10, 1890.

The Chicago Massacre of 1812. Chicago: The Dibble Publishing Company, 1893.

The History of Chicago. Edited by John Moses and Joseph Kirkland. 2 vols. Chicago: Munsell Publishing Company, 1895.

Reprint

Zury: The Meanest Man in Spring County, Facsimile Reprint with an Introduction by John T. Flanagan. Urbana: University of Illinois Press, 1956. Reprint is of the 1887 edition of the novel.

Contributions to Magazines

"The Horn of Scarcity," *America*, I (September 20, 1886), 6.

"The Captain of Company K," *America*, I (May 26, 1888), 6 ff.

"Under Fire," *America*, I (December 20, 1888), 19 ff.

"Christmas a Quarter Century Ago," *America*, I (December 20, 1888), 9 ff.

"Hanging is a Painless Death," *America*, I (January 17, 1889), 9 ff.

"The Owl and The Newspaper Man," *America*, V (June 22, 1891), 476-77.

"An Experiment in Play-Writing," *Atlantic Monthly*, XLIV (August, 1879), 149-55.

"Lorna Doone" (A Review of R. D. Blackmoore's *Lorna Doone*), *Bookbuyer*, II (1883), 429-31.

"The Lady or the Tiger? or Both," *Century Magazine*, XXIV (June, 1883), 318-19.

"A Historic Trial," *Chicago Tribune*, August 21, 1886.

"A Letter on the Roelle Junker & Company Case," *Chicago Tribune*, January 27, 1887.

"Letters of Joseph Kirkland, Special Correspondent with the Warner G. Miller Party," *Chicago Tribune*, April 5, 8, 19, 24, 29; May 3, 10, 17, 24, 31; June 7, 1891.

"Was Its Best Fencer," *Chicago Sunday Tribune*, May 27, 1894.

"The Chicago Fair," *Critic*, XVIII (November, 1893), 337 ff.

"Zury's Soft Spot," *Contributors' Magazine*, February 24, 1893, pp. 32-34.

"One Clergyman and One Suburban Serving Maid," *Contributors' Magazine*, May 16, 1894.

"The Memoirs of Madam D'Arblay" (A review of *The Diary and Letters of Frances Burney, Madame D'Arblay*, edited by Sarah Woolsey), *Dial*, I (June, 1880), 30-35.

"Curiosities and Humors of the Law" (A review of Benjamin Abbott's *Judge and Jury*), *Dial*, I (August, 1880), 67-69.

"A Partisan Romance" (A review of Albion Tourgee's *Bricks Without Straw*), *Dial*, I (October, 1880), 110-12.

"The Chinese Question" (A review of George F. Seward's *Chinese Immigration*), *Dial*, I (March, 1881), 233-36.

"The Talleyrand Letters" (A review of *The Correspondence of Prince Talleyrand and King Louis XVIII During the Congress of Vienna*), *Dial*, II (July, 1881), 57-59.

"Lincoln, Stanton and McClellan" (A review of George B. McClellan's *The Peninsular Campaign of General McClellan*), *Dial*, II (September, 1881), 93-94.

"Anthony Trollope's Autobiography," *Dial*, IV (December, 1883), 190-92.

"Tolstoi and the Russian Invasion of the Realm of Fiction" (A review of Part III of *War and Peace*), *Dial*, VII (August, 1886), 79-81.

"The Second Corps of the Army of the Potomac" (A review of F. A. Walker's *History of the Second Army Corps in the Army of the Potomac*), *Dial*, VII (April, 1887), 285-88.

"Patrick Henry" (A review of Moses C. Tyler's *Patrick Henry*), *Dial*, VIII (October, 1887), 19-21.

"The Fighting Veres" (A review of Charles B. Mackham's *Lives of Sir Francis and Sir Horace Vere*), *Dial*, VIII (April, 1888), 288-90.

"The Dreadful Truth About Napoleon" (A review of L. A. F. de Bourrienne's *Memories of Napoleon Bonaparte*), *Dial,* X (October, 1889), 125-27.

"An Introduction to Uncle Dick Wootton's *The Pioneer Frontiersman of the Rocky Mountain Range,*" *Dial,* XI (March, 1890), 312.

"Realism Versus Other Isms," *Dial,* XIV (February 16, 1893), 99-101.

"An Inside View of Waterloo" (A review of John C. Rope's *The Campaign of Waterloo*), *Dial,* XIV (May 1, 1893), 275-78.

"Zury's $1000 Blunder," *Ehrich's Quarterly* (October, 1887).

"Meet and Fitting," *Figaro,* V (March, 1892), 168 ff.

"Tell the Sentry to Load with Balls," *Figaro,* V (March, 1892), 47-48.

"Peg Leg Sullivan," *Figaro,* V (May, 1892), 168-69.

"The Surgeon's Miracle," McClure's Magazine, September, 1893, pp. 555-56.

"An Account of the Chicago Fire," *New England Monthly Magazine,* VI (August, 1892), 726-42.

"Atlantic Home," *St. Nicholas,* July, 1882, p. 19.

"Among the Poor in Chicago," *Scribner's Magazine,* XII (July, 1892), 3-27.

Manuscript Materials

Kirkland Papers, Newberry Library, Chicago, Illinois:
"The Dummy," manuscript of a farce for private theatricals; "The Little End of the Horn," a poem, exercise in versification; "Double Charades," a dramatic sketch; Joseph Kirkland's Scrapbook; "Glorious Eyes," a poem; "Blinded," a poem; incomplete untitled poem on bankruptcy; incomplete poem on Mammoth Cave; "Jake," an incomplete poem; autobiographical sketch of Joseph Kirkland; journal fragment.

Unpublished Material in the Possession of Winifred Wilson, Evanston, Illinois:
Copy of Memorial to Joseph Kirkland, by Mark Bangs, and written at the time of Kirkland's death; Memorial by Thomas Bryan to Joseph Kirkland, May 1, 1894; letter of Cordelia Kirkland to Louise Kirkland Sanborn, April 21, 1917; Hamlin Garland to Winifred Wilson, June 3, 1927; Hobart Chatfield-Taylor to Winifred Wilson, June 7, 1927; Jean Stansbury Holden (Mrs. E. G. Holden) to Winifred Wilson, May 27, 1927; General Joseph Kirkland to his son William, May, 1839; Lucas Nebeker to Winifred Wilson, February 29, 1926; sketch of the life of Caroline

Selected Bibliography

Kirkland written by her granddaughter Cordelia Kirkland; records of conversations with Louise Kirkland Sanborn (This mass of material is very large. It covers a vast number of subjects and is useful in showing Louise Kirkland Sanborn's opinions of her father, Joseph Kirkland.); a longhand copy of a flyleaf from a family Bible with the dates of the births of the Kirkland children; and copies of all material found in the Kirkland Papers, Newberry Library.

Material from Other Sources

The Prairie Chicken, I, Nos. 1-12 (October 1, 1864-September 1, 1865). Photostatic copy in possession of the author. Two files of the periodical are extant, one in the Chicago Public Library and one in the New York Public Library. (I have followed Mabbott and Jordan in my use of the work as a manuscript.)

Letter of Joseph Kirkland to Judge Ackerman, August 5, 1858. In the files of the Illinois Central Railroad, Chicago, Illinois.

Letter of Joseph Kirkland to the Adjutant General, February 22, 1863. In the Department of Records, Office of the Adjutant General, Department of Army, Washington, D.C.

Letters of Joseph Kirkland to Hamlin Garland, May 23, 25, 31, 1887; June 7, September 16, November 14, 1887; February 13, March 20, 24, 26, 28, May 3, 16, 1888. Copies made from transcripts in the possession of Eldon C. Hill, Oxford, Ohio, in whose possession the originals were placed by Garland before his death. Professor Hill returned the letters to Garland's daughter after the father's death. Copies in the Kirkland Papers.

Public Documents

Adjutant General's Report, Illinois. Vol. I. Springfield: n. p., 1867. Gives Kirkland's war record.

Records of the Circuit Court, Danville, Illinois, Box 28, Document 1; Box 32, Documents 1-5. The records of Kirkland's trial as cosigner of a note for C. E. English.

U. S. Congress, Senate. *Senate Document, No. 37.* Parts 1 and 2, 46th Congress, 1st Session. Washington: Government Printing Office, 1879. The record of Kirkland's army service.

Vermilion County, Illinois, *Register of Deeds,* Vols. VIII, XII, XXIX, XXXIV, XLIV, LIV, LXXVIII, and CXXII. The records of Kirkland's purchase and sale of coal-mining lands.

War of the Rebellion, Official Records, Series I. Published under the direction of the Secretary of War. Vols. VI, XI, XIX, and

XXI. Washington: Government Printing Office, 1880-1881. The official records of Kirkland's promotions in the army.

Newspapers

Boston Transcript, May 16, 1887. The Garland review of *Zury.* April 30, 1894. The notice of Kirkland's death.

Chicago Daily News, October 26, 1926. The notice of the death of John Meeker, prototype for Zury Prouder.

Chicago Tribune, January 2, 12, 14, 16, 18; September 1, 12; December 20, 1875: notices of social, literary and musical events in Chicago in which Kirkland took part. January 1, 1876: Kirkland's letter about a law case. September 14, November 7, 10, 1877: notice of Kirkland's work on the savings banks of Chicago. December 9, 11, 13, 14, 1877: notices of Kirkland's play and its run. April 30, 1894: notice of Kirkland's death.

Detroit Free Press, September 22, 29, 1899; June 8, 1890. Notices of the literary contest which Kirkland won with his *Captain of Company K.*

New York Tribune, September 30, 1888. Review of *The McVeys.*

SECONDARY SOURCES

CADY, EDWIN. *The Road to Realism: The Early Years, 1837-1885, of William Dean Howells.* Syracuse, N. Y.: Syracuse University Press, 1957. The first volume of a definitive study of Howells.

————. *The Realist at War: The Mature Years, 1885-1920, of William Dean Howells.* Syracuse, N. Y.: Syracuse University Press, 1959. The second volume of a definitive study of Howells.

CARTER, EVERETT. *Howells and the Rise of Realism.* Philadelphia and New York: J. B. Lippincott Company, 1954. A careful, thoughtful study of realism as a literary theory.

DONDORE, DOROTHY A. *The Prairie and the Making of Middle America.* Cedar Rapids, Iowa: The Torch Press, 1926. Suggestive, but needs additions and corrections.

DUFFY, BERNARD. *The Chicago Renaissance in American Letters, A Critical History.* East Lansing: Michigan State University Press, 1954. Includes a good summary of Kirkland's work.

FLANAGAN, JOHN T. "Joseph Kirkland, Pioneer Realist," *American Literature,* XI (November, 1939), 273-84. The first good summary of Kirkland's importance in Midwest realism.

————. "A Note on Joseph Kirkland," *American Literature,* XII (March, 1940), 107-8. Additional information on Kirkland's work.

HENSON, CLYDE E. "Joseph Kirkland's Novels," *Journal of the Illinois State Historical Society,* XLIV (Summer, 1951), 42-46. A summary of Kirkland's novels and the Illinois setting.

————. "Joseph Kirkland's Influence on Hamlin Garland," *American Literature,* XIII, No. 4 (January, 1952), 458-63. The Kirkland-Garland correspondence.

————. "The Life and Work of Joseph Kirkland." Unpublished Ph.D. Dissertation, Western Reserve University, 1950.

HOLADAY, CLAYTON A. "Joseph Kirkland: Biography and Criticism." Unpublished Ph.D. dissertation, Indiana University, 1950. A good study of Kirkland.

————. "Kirkland's *Captain of Company K*: A Twice Told Tale," *American Literature,* XX (1956), 62-66. A study of parts of the novel which Kirkland sold as short stories.

HOLLOWAY, JEAN. *Hamlin Garland, A Biography.* Austin: University of Texas Press, 1960. The best study of Garland and his work.

KAZIN, ALFRED. *On Native Grounds.* New York: Harcourt, Brace and Company, 1942. A fine study of American fiction from the time of the struggle for realism. Abridged as a Doubleday Anchor Book. Garden City, New York: Doubleday and Company, 1956.

LA BUDDE, KENNETH. "A Note on the Text of Joseph Kirkland's *Zury*," *American Literature,* XX (January, 1949), 452-55. A comparison of the texts of the two editions of *Zury.*

LEASE, BENJAMIN. "Realism and Joseph Kirkland's *Zury*," *American Literature,* XXIII, No. 4 (January, 1952), 464-66. A study of Kirkland's use of sex in his novel.

LEWIS, LLOYD. "Letters of A Pioneer Realist," *The Newberry Library Bulletin,* No. 3 (December, 1945), 3-7. A discussion of the Kirkland Papers in the Newberry Library.

LOCKWOOD, LUCY. *The Frontier in American Literature.* New York: Thomas Y. Crowells Company, 1927. Suggestive in its comments on the Turner thesis and literature.

MABBOTT, THOMAS O. and JORDAN, PHILIP D. "The Prairie Chicken." *Journal of the Illinois State Historical Society,* XV (October, 1932), 155 ff. Recounts the discovery in the New York Public Library of a file of the newspaper.

RUSK, RALPH L. *The Literature of the Middle Western Frontier.* 2 vols. New York: Columbia University Press, 1925. An exhaustive bibliography.

SMITH, HENRY NASH. *Virgin Land, The American West as Symbol and Myth*. Cambridge: Harvard University Press, 1950. A superb study, both in method and scope, of the quest of the American for his own identity.

SOLOMAN, ERIC. "Another Analogue for *The Red Badge of Courage*," *Nineteenth Century Fiction*, XIII (1958), 63-65. Points to parallel situations in Kirkland's war novel and Crane's work.

Index

Names of characters and places in Kirkland's works are followed by the title—in parentheses—of the work in which they appear.

Realism in fiction, 83-88
Religion in Kirkland's fiction, 114-16
Roosevelt, Theodore, 132; *The Winning of the West;* 132
Runnion, James B., 72

Sanborn, Louise Kirkland (daughter of Joseph), 31, 43, 58, 129
Sanborn, Victor, 129
Sanders, Dolly and Jim (*The Mc-Veys*), 120, 122-23
Saracen Club, 75
Sartain, John, 27
Scribner's Magazine, 80
Shields, John, 65
Smith, Henry Nash, 117
Sparrow, Anne, *also* Anne McVey, Anne Prouder (*Zury; The Mc-Veys; The Captain of Company K*), 89, 91, 92, 93, 94, 95, 109-12, 118, 119, 121, 128, 141
Spirit of the Times, 32
Springville (*Zury; The McVeys*), 119, 120, 121
Stafford, Dr. (*The McVeys; The Captain of Company K*), 119, 120, 121, 128
Stansbury, Elizabeth, 19
Stansbury, Joseph, 29, 58
Stansbury, Samuel, 42, 43
Stedman, E. C., 135
Swing, Reverend David, 72

Taine, Hippolyte, 16, 86
Thorborn (*The Captain of Company K*), 125, 126
Thoreau, Henry David, 30, 32
Tolstoy, Leo, 78, 79, 84, 87, 93
Turner, Frederick Jackson, 85
Twain, Mark, 101, 111
Twentieth Century Club, 75

Union Magazine of Literature and Art, 27

Van Doren, Carl, 117

Walk-in-the-Water, 17
Wallack, Fanny, 31
Wallack's Lyceum, 31
Warner, Charles Dudley, 30, 75
Wayback (*Zury*), 21, 99
Webster, General, 65, 68
Wentworth, John, 135, 136
Westerner in literature, 26
Whiskey ring scandal, 65-68
Whitman, Walt, 31
Wilkinson, Dorothy, 118
Wilkinson, Dudley, 61
Wilkinson, John, 39, 43, 129
Willard, Frances, 135
Willie (*Zury*), 95
Wilson, Winifred, 15

Zola, Emile, 84, 85, 87